GEOLOGY AND ARC
BERKSHI

for people who aren't geologists or
archæologists

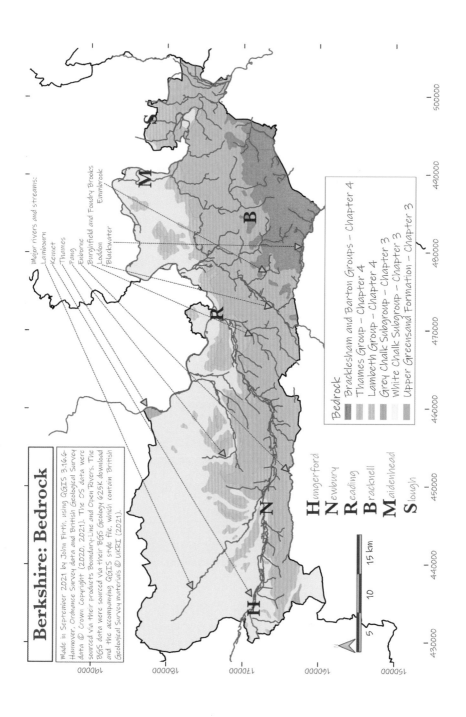

Berkshire: Bedrock

Made in September 2021 by John Firth, using QGIS 3.16.6-Hannover. Ordnance Survey data and British Geological Survey data © Crown Copyright (2020, 2021). The OS data were sourced via their products Boundary-Line and Open Rivers. The BGS data were sourced via their BGS Geology 625K download and the accompanying QGIS style file, which contain British Geological Survey materials © UKRI (2021).

Major rivers and streams:
Lambourn
Kennet
Thames
Pang
Enborne
Burghfield and Foudry Brooks
Loddon
Blackwater
Emmbrook

Hungerford
Newbury
Reading
Bracknell
Maidenhead
Slough

Bedrock
Bracklesham and Barton Groups – Chapter 4
Thames Group – Chapter 4
Lambeth Group – Chapter 4
Grey Chalk Subgroup – Chapter 3
White Chalk Subgroup – Chapter 3
Upper Greensand Formation – Chapter 3

5   10   15 km

150000   160000   170000   180000   190000

430000   440000   450000   460000   470000   480000   490000   500000

GEOLOGY AND ARCHÆOLOGY OF BERKSHIRE

for people who aren't geologists or archæologists

John Firth

Baffin Books

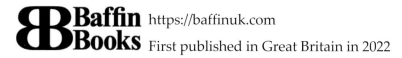 https://baffinuk.com

First published in Great Britain in 2022

British Library Cataloguing Data
A CIP record for this book is available from the
British Library

ISBN 978-1-9998198-8-0

First impression

Printed and bound by Biddles Books Ltd,
Castle House, East Winch Road, Blackborough End, King's Lynn,
Norfolk PE32 1SF
www.biddles.co.uk

Contents

Maps and Diagrams

Photographs

Introduction

THE VISIBLE GEOLOGY OF THE COUNTY is recent in geological terms, being mostly sediments laid down during the last 150 million years. Below the surface, seismic surveys have found Ordovician sedimentary rocks (perhaps 450 million years old – *see Appendix 2 for a list of geological periods*) that were extensively folded and faulted during the Devonian period (which began nearly 420 million years ago and lasted for around 60 million years). Boreholes have found rocks that date back to the early Devonian. Perhaps 80 million years later some limestone and coal were laid down during the Carboniferous period, and some volcanic rocks probably date from that period. (I have not been able to find out whether these were thrown out then by a volcano we have not been able to find, or intruded later into gaps or cracks below the surface.) There follows another gap in the record, of 40 to 70 million years, covering most of the Permian period and much of the Triassic. This we can explain – *see Chapter 2*. For the 100 million years or so after that (Jurassic and early Cretaceous rocks) the record is spotty, because not many boreholes have been sunk that deeply. Most of the bedrock we know about in Berkshire dates from the Cretaceous period, when the chalk started to be laid down.

Neither is the more recent rock record continuous. Several layers were laid down at different times during the Palæogene period (notably, the Reading Formation) but these have often been eroded away over high ground, or where rivers have cut through them. In particular, the London clay covers much of Berkshire, but the thickness can vary a great deal, sometimes over very short distances. In contrast, almost nothing survives from the Neogene period that followed it, although the Quaternary period – the last 2.5 million years – has made major marks on the landscape.

However, these are not really 'gaps' in the rock record. A motto widely quoted in geological circles is 'the present is a guide to the past'. Around the world we can see new rock being laid down (or pushed up by volcanoes or earth movements) at the same time that surface rock is being eroded by wind, water and quarrying. There is quite a lot of sand, gravel and clay in Berkshire, and all three are often produced by erosion of older rocks. The British Isles were not always where they are now; the rocks we can find tell us that Berkshire spent long ages under water, and sometimes the absence of rocks tells us that Berkshire spent long ages above the sea but in desert latitudes. Were there any economic reason to dig down and look for them, much older rocks will lie below the Devonian rocks that we have found in boreholes. Closer to the surface, rocks from the Jurassic – like those we can see in Oxfordshire, just a few miles away – might once have covered Berkshire; some are still present at depth, as are Triassic rocks, here and there.

No metamorphic rocks have been found in (or below) Berkshire. Metamorphism in rocks is mostly a result of heat and pressure, so tends to happen deep underground. It can happen at the surface as a result of sudden shock, such as a meteor impact, but there is no evidence of a meteor strike of any size in Berkshire. It can also happen when rock comes into contact with much hotter rocks. Some volcanic (igneous) rocks have been found but none of the structures that mark an active or extinct volcano are now present, so (as I wrote earlier) how these rocks were laid down (or intruded) is a bit of a mystery. Another factor causing or contributing to metamorphism (and volcanic activity) is the movement of tectonic plates, and this has certainly left its mark on Berkshire.

Geology sometimes seems like long and complicated lists of 'what happened when'. There are potentially four-and-a-half billion years since the Earth was formed (we currently believe), so potentially there is a lot of 'when'; the further back we look, the less 'what' we will find and the more confusing it is to try to make sense of it. Fortunately, plate tectonics, the theory that represents how we currently believe the lands and seas on our planet were formed and may ultimately be destroyed and reformed in some other configuration, offers a convincing way to look at what 'happened' might mean. In this book I will try to summarise what geologists believe was happening during the periods in which rocks and other deposits were formed in Berkshire, to try to explain what we can see today.

So, before I go on to describe what can be seen, and where, I will outline plate tectonics *(see below and Appendix 1)*. This will help me explain how Berkshire's geology came about *(in Chapters 2 to 5)*, and put into perspective what we can see and what we can infer from the evidence provided by the many hundreds of boreholes that have been dug in Berkshire. Finally, *in Chapter 6* I will look at human presence in Berkshire – Thatcham, and possibly Kintbury, may be the oldest settlements in the UK.

It is important to bear in mind that the rivers that in some ways define Berkshire have not always run where we see them now. Until after the Anglian ice age *(see Chapter 5* – quite recently, in geological terms) the Thames did not run through Berkshire; the Kennet, the Loddon and the Blackwater, too, are comparatively recent rivers that have changed their courses, perhaps as a result of the changes in the course of the Thames (which will have affected how rain drains off the hills in the west and north of the county).

Human (and proto-human) activity in the recent and distant past can be studied through what humans (and proto-humans) leave behind them (archæology). I have not studied palæontology (life before human dominance of the planet), though I do mention fossils in a few places.

Some technical vocabulary is unavoidable in a scientific subject, so a glossary is given at the back of this book, along with a list of resources and a few other materials, if you would like to study geology and archæology (or just Berkshire's geology and archæology) further. Words **in bold** are explained in the glossary. I wrote this book in part to teach myself about geology and archæology, and it is written for people like me who are interested in the subjects but not expert in them. Where I hoped I could avoid technical words I have done so. This might mean that I have missed some points, got others wrong and over-simplified where I should have spelled out, and I would be glad to learn where this book could be improved, in case it ever runs to another edition.

Plate tectonics

This section is only an outline of the theory: *I've included a little more detail and some diagrams in Appendix 1.* Anyone interested to know more may like to read Graham Park's *Introducing Tectonics, Rock Structures and Mountain Belts* (Edinburgh: Dunedin Academic Press, 2012) or some of the more general books listed in the References.

The Earth's radius is roughly 6,370km and our planet has four concentric layers. We walk on the surface of the crust *(see below)*; beneath it is a solid mantle that is approximately 2,900km thick; then an outer core of liquid iron and nickel that is about 2,100km thick; and in the centre a solid inner core made of the same materials, that is roughly two-thirds the size of the Moon. The crust is made of 'superficial' layers (in Berkshire, soil, sand, clay or gravel), on top of layers of 'bedrock' laid down at different times. (Bedrock can be hard rock like granite or limestone, soft rock like chalk, or materials we might not regard as rock, such as sand or clay.) While the average thickness of the Earth's crust is probably around 20km, it is much thinner under the oceans and can be much thicker under (say) mountain ranges. The crust rests on the mantle, and so the mantle is much closer to ground level where the crust is thin, and may even break through it (as some types of volcano do).

The crust and the top 100km or so of the mantle together form the **lithosphere**. The lithosphere operates in many ways as a unit; but the crust's rocks are much less dense than mantle rocks. Rocks nearer the surface are cooler than the rocks below them and, as depth increases, so does pressure from the rocks above. The lithosphere forms fourteen major plates (and a large number of microplates) that move slowly past, over or under one another, causing oceans to open and close, continents to form and break up, mountains to rise and the floors of rifts to fall. They can move because heat and pressure cause the rocks that make up the **asthenosphere** (the next 300km or so of the mantle) to deform more easily than the rocks above them. Sometimes this deformation is a kind of flow (over long periods the rocks change shape) and at other times it happens violently (when rocks break).

There are three main tectonic processes: rifting and spreading, **subduction** and parallel movement. **Constructive** movement sees two plates move apart, creating a rift that gradually spreads, **destructive** movement sees one plate subducted beneath another – passed back into the mantle to be recycled – and **conservative** movement sees one plate slide past another. Movement might be 'pushed' (for example, where new rock rising from the asthenosphere pushes through faults to erupt as a volcano) or 'pulled' (by gravity drawing rock towards the centre of the Earth). A fault is a place where the rock has broken and one or both sides of the break have moved: in opposite directions (**transcurrent faults**), where one side of the fault has fallen (**normal faults**) or where one side has been pushed upwards (**reverse faults**). It can follow a boundary between two plates, or cut across, and can change direction.

1

Berkshire: a bird's-eye view

BERKSHIRE IS MADE UP OF a relatively rural west and an increasingly urban east explained by its hills and rivers (*see Figure 1.1, over the page*).

The Thames that forms its north-eastern boundary and the Kennet that flows from the south-west to join the Thames at Reading have been the most important of the rivers for human beings, but (from west to east) the Lambourn, the Pang, the Loddon and the Blackwater (among others) all attracted human settlement. I will turn to this subject *in Chapter 6*.

The western end of the county lies over the Berkshire **syncline** *(see Chapter 2, Figure 2.2)*, and the whole county is shaped by the north-western limb of the London Basin 'synform' that forms the Chilterns (and further west, the Berkshire Downs).* Chalk and later deposits have filled both synforms.

West Berkshire's geological basement was probably formed in the early Devonian or late Silurian periods, then folded during the Carboniferous period *(see Chapter 2)*. The county's near-surface geology was washed off the London Platform during the Cretaceous period *(see Chapter 3)* then shaped in two significant stages; first the Alpine **orogeny** which formed the London Basin *(see Chapter 4)*, and later by the Anglian glaciation *(see Chapter 5)*. The Anglian and later glaciations moved the course of the Thames southwards, and brought sands, clays and gravels down the rivers that have defined the county's human history *(see Chapter 6)*. Some iron was washed down with these deposits. The British Geological Survey (BGS) map of Berkshire Mineral Resources shows 'few rocks that are suitable

---

* A syncline is, essentially, a bowl; the London Basin is more like a vast valley running out into the North Sea; hence, a 'synform'.

for building stone', 'poor… hydrocarbon prospectivity' and 'thin' and 'unprospective' coalbeds, but brick and other clays, chalk (for agricultural lime) and some 14.2 million tonnes of sands and gravels.

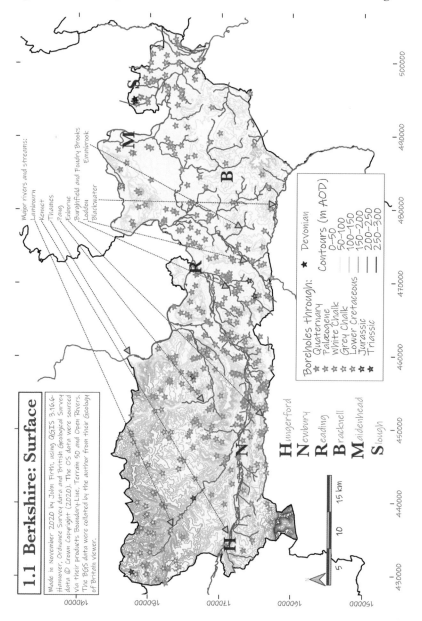

1.1 Berkshire: Surface

Made in November 2020 by John Firth, using QGIS 3.16.6-Hannover, Ordnance Survey data and British Geological Survey data © Crown Copyright (2020). The OS data were sourced via their products Boundary-Line, Terrain 50 and Open Rivers. The BGS data were collated by the author from their Geology of Britain viewer.

Major rivers and streams:
Lambourn
Kennet
Thames
Pang
Enborne
Burghfield and Foudry Brooks
Loddon
Emmbrook
Blackwater

Boreholes through:
Quaternary
Palaeogene
White Chalk
Grey Chalk
Lower Cretaceous
Jurassic
Triassic

★ Devonian

Contours (m AOD)
0–50
50–100
100–150
150–200
200–250
250–300

H ungerford
N ewbury
R eading
B racknell
M aidenhead
S lough

0   5   10   15 km

(The BGS map was prepared in 2001; but as these sands and gravels were then being extracted at a rate of 1.1 million tonnes a year, perhaps this resource is running out. The most recent figure I have found was 615,000 tonnes extracted in 2007.) Not mentioned by the BGS, there are also flint and 'sarsens' *(see Chapter 4)*.

I collated BGS data for 492 boreholes in Berkshire (for the distribution, *see Figure 1.1*). Few of these went much more than 30 or 40 metres into the ground. The following graph collates data from seventeen of the boreholes, which I will be referring to in detail in the chapters that follow:

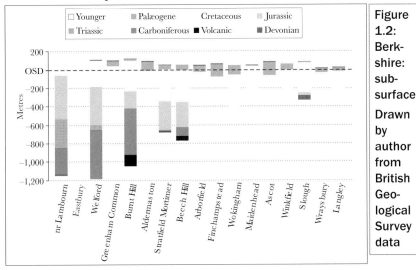

Figure 1.2: Berkshire: sub-surface Drawn by author from British Geological Survey data

The first thing to note is that little is now in place that was laid down:

◊ after the Palæogene period that ran from about 66 million years ago to about 20 million years ago *(discussed in Chapter 5)* or

◊ during the Triassic, which ran from about 251 million years ago for about 50 million years and

◊ nothing survives from the 52-million-year Permian period that preceded the Triassic – *see Chapter 2*.

Some of these periods lasted longer than others (*see Appendix 2 for details*), but even so the thickness of the Cretaceous layers that remain (principally, chalk) is much more consistent across the county than the thickness of the surviving Palæogene layers above them or Jurassic, Triassic and Carboniferous layers below them. (Please note: six of the boreholes in Figure 1.2 were only sunk a little way into the chalk so no Cretaceous layers appear beneath them; five were not sunk very far past it, so for them the column stops at the Cretaceous; and we have no idea how thick the Devonian layers below Lambourn or Slough are, but as these are the only Devonian rocks found in Berkshire so far, I thought it was important to record them on the graph.)

The following summary of the BGS data I collated might interest some readers:

Periods:	Jurassic and older	Cretaceous			Palæo-gene	Quater-nary
		below chalk	Grey Chalk	White Chalk		
Found in (of 492 boreholes):	2%	4%	13%	93%	70%	72%
Thickest:	1,071 metres	126 metres	104 metres	246 metres	184 metres	15 metres
Narrowest:	18 metres	6.2 metres	8 metres	18 metres	1 metre	<1 metre
Median:	227 metres	78 metres	69 metres	81 metres	31 metres	4 metres

Please note that for the last three rows of this table I only included layers if the borehole penetrated to the layer beneath, and I also excluded boreholes that did not penetrate below at least one Palæogene layer. In other words, those rows take into account layers for which we know the total thickness, for boreholes that found at least one Palæogene or older layer. A total of 390 boreholes met these criteria. In the table, 'thickest' and 'narrowest' include all beds of this age found in a single borehole; 'thickest means greatest total and 'narrowest' means smallest total.

2

What may have shaped Berkshire's geology

IT IS BELIEVED THAT THE FIRST CONTINENT, Rodinia, formed about 1.1 billion years ago and started to break up about 750 million years ago. One major fragment was called Gondwana, and over the next 300 million years (i.e. by the middle of the Ordovician **period**) it separated from two other fragments, Laurentia and Baltica, as an ocean opened up between them that geologists have named the Iapetus Ocean.

Throughout this period most of what now forms Scotland and Northern Ireland was part of Laurentia, and not far from the equator, while what now forms England, Wales, Ireland and some of lowland Scotland was part of Gondwana, and some 60° south (within what is now the Antarctic circle). There was no ice at the South Pole then, so the world's sea level was a great

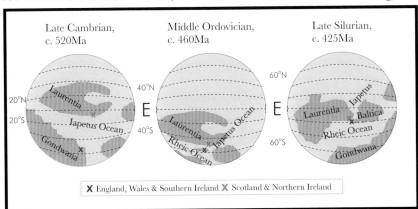

Late Cambrian, c. 520Ma   Middle Ordovician, c. 460Ma   Late Silurian, c. 425Ma

X England, Wales & Southern Ireland **X** Scotland & Northern Ireland

Figure 2.1: How the British Isles came to be

Redrawn by the author from Toghill, 2000

deal higher. The eastern seaboard of Laurentia and the northern seaboard of Gondwana were both under water: both deep-ocean and shallower, continental-shelf sediments form part of Britain's Precambrian basement.

In the Cambrian period (from approximately 544 million years ago) fossil evidence for life on Earth becomes (relatively) plentiful, providing evidence we can correlate with data on the mineralogy of surrounding rocks (crystal structures and chemistry), type (e.g. igneous, sedimentary), ages and **palæomagnetism**. As a result, much more can be surmised about the Cambrian period than about earlier ones; the sketch maps *in Figure 2.1* give a rough idea of what is believed to have happened.

The Iapetus Ocean began to close (which may have taken 100 million years), dragging Laurentia southwards, very slowly. A new Rheic Ocean began to open, separating a small sliver called Avalonia from Gondwana and driving it north, much faster. Avalonia contained southern Britain and parts of what is now Labrador, and may have been more like a chain of islands separated by shallow channels than a continent. About 440 million years ago the South Pole (which was then part of Gondwana) entered an ice age, causing sea levels to fall. Areas of England may have risen above water, although when the Gondwanan ice eventually melted (during the Silurian period) marine transgressions occurred. By this, geologists mean that the sea may have risen and spread across the land, then retreated, possibly several times.

During the same Silurian period Avalonia collided with Baltica, folding Ordovician rocks across southern England. Around that time or perhaps 40 million years later (different views are current) the combined landmass met Laurentia at about 20° south, fusing Scotland and Northern Ireland to the rest of Britain and Ireland. This second collision threw up the Caledonian mountains that covered Scotland, northern England and north and west Wales. The continent thus created is sometimes called the 'Old Red Sandstone' continent, for reasons that will become clear. The Rheic Ocean continued to open, driving the continent north – from what is now the southern desert belt across the equator. Both dry heat and the humid, rainy conditions typical of tropical latitudes tend to break rock down quickly; as the continent moved out of the southern desert belt, north through the tropics and out into the northern desert belt the new Caledonian mountains eroded and the remains were deposited as thick, hard, sedimentary layers over the whole country: the Old Red Sandstone. **Outcrops** of the Old Red Sandstone (rock that is visible at the surface) can be seen in the north and the midlands – west Gloucestershire is probably the nearest outcrop to Berkshire.

The oldest rocks found by boreholes in Berkshire belong to the Lower Old Red Sandstone, which is believed to have been laid down between 380 and 420 million years ago. They are in two clusters: around 1,300metres beneath the Berkshire Downs near Lambourn, where they lie beneath one rim of the Berkshire syncline *(see later in this chapter)* and around 325metres beneath Slough and Langley *(see Chapter 1, Figure 1.2)*. A third cluster at Sonning is technically in Oxfordshire so not included in this book.

Berkshire probably remained under water for around 80 million years: a coastal area or shallow shelf sea during the Silurian, increasingly covered by the Rheic Ocean during the Devonian period. To the north and east, a Wales–London–Brabant **massif** was pushed up and out of the sea, and great thicknesses of eroded sediment must have washed off it, some of which underlies the east of the county as a thin band of (early Carboniferous) limestone that was laid down before being uplifted. Most of this has been eroded away in its turn, the earliest of many **unconformities** in the region (layers present in neighbouring areas that either were never laid down in Berkshire, or have since been worn away).

This huge span of time saw the south polar icecap melt, the vast proto-Pacific Ocean grow, generating new ocean floor that may have raised sea levels around the world, and the Rheic Ocean close. This closing drove many fragments of Rodinia to join again, to form Pangæa. In what we call the Variscan orogeny, this collision drove up a belt of fold mountains running from what are now the

Appalachians through south-west Britain and central Europe to the Urals (although Britain has no mountains from this period, so perhaps was on a **conservative plate boundary**).

Seas, seashores and sediments

Many sedimentary rocks are formed from deposits brought to where they are now by water. As much of the rest of this book will be looking at sedimentary rocks and other deposits that were laid down on coasts, just offshore and deeper below the sea, let us look at some of the processes involved.

A coast might be a simple boundary between land and sea – a cliff, say – or something more complex, such as a delta or a saltmarsh. Rivers join the sea at coasts, bringing stones, **sand, silt, clay** and organic remains from inland which spread out in front of the river's mouth in an alluvial 'fan': the alluvial fan from a big river such as the Thames can be vast. Typically larger, heavier material will be deposited sooner than finer, lighter material that the flow can carry further; chemical reactions (where fresh water meets salt water) can affect this process. Tides wash material inshore and carry material out; when they approach the coast at an angle they can move material along it (a process known as longshore drift). Like rivers, tides tend to move finer, lighter material further than larger, heavier material. Coasts are subject to weathering just like everywhere else: heat, wind, rain, snow and ice, aided by salt, wear down or break up surface rock and carry loose material out to sea, filling up inshore areas to create marshes and deltas or add to those that rivers have created. Storms disrupt these processes: winds, rain and strong waves break up solid surfaces and carry material further. Earthquakes and landslides, which happen under water, on land and at coasts, are other types of disruption.

So, whether simple or complex, a coast is a boundary *area*, not a boundary *line*, usually forming a shelf that eventually falls into deep sea. The coastal shelf can be narrow and steep or wide and gradual; because it is shallower than open sea or deep ocean it tends to be warmed by sunshine and a large range of plants and animals live there (corals are a good example of the latter). When they die, they leave their remains on the shelf. So, as well as material carried off the land – stones, sand, silt, clay and organic remains, growing progressively finer the further offshore – coastal shelf sediments can include the remains of the plants and animals that live there, and some material carried in from the open sea by the tides. By contrast, deep seabeds tend to be occupied by few or no plants and relatively few, highly specialised animals. Sedimentation is continuous in the deep sea and the sediments laid down there tend to be muds washed off the land (which have travelled a long way, so are very fine), volcanic ash (and, near volcanoes, lava) and the shells, skeletons and other remains of animals, most of which are microscopic.

These differences between river-mouth, beach, coastal shelf and deep-sea sediments will crop up regularly in this book. I discuss clay *in Chapter 4* and gravel *in Chapter 5*; 'sand' describes particles between 0.062 and 2mm in diameter, which might be quartz or a range of minerals or organic materials (e.g. shell). 'Mud' is not a technical term but a useful way of talking about (usually) mixtures of clay, silt, soil and gravel.

Over geological time, sea level is affected by global temperatures (warmer water occupies a greater volume than cooler water and the volume is greatly affected by how much water is bound up in ice). The local impact of sea level is affected by changes in ground level (tectonic movements can stretch continents, creating great plains; compress them, sending up mountain ranges; and fold them, creating domes and basins).

The Berkshire syncline

BGS maps show several faults in the south and west of the county and a Berkshire syncline in the north-west: beneath the geography we can see, the Devonian and earlier layers have been pushed upwards by more than 700metres to form a long, elliptical groove running from Maidenhead for more than 100km west-north-westwards, up beneath what is now the Ridgeway towards Aston Tirrold in Oxfordshire.

In Figures 2.2 and 2.3 I try to give an idea of the part of the syncline that is within Berkshire: as it continues into Oxfordshire the Carboniferous layers (and the Devonian layers beneath them) continue to rise. Figure 2.2 is my projection, based on the layers found in twelve boreholes (the lines show what was found in each hole; I explain below what I think is happening at Burnt Hill). It names the deeper boreholes; for the locations of the shallower ones, *please see Figure 1.2*. The cross-section runs a little southwards of west–east, roughly along the long axis of the syncline, then turns northwards between Wokingham and Maidenhead (included to give an idea of the syncline's rim). My projection does not match what was found in the Burnt Hill borehole, where the Carboniferous

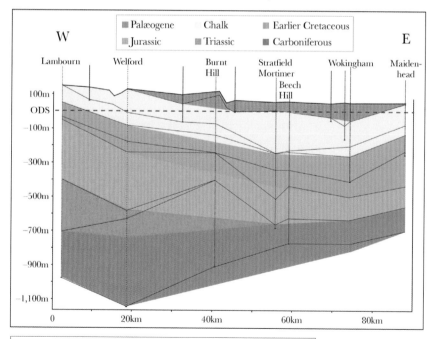

Figure 2.2: Cross-section along the Berkshire syncline
Drawn by author from British Geological Survey data

and Triassic layers are found much closer to the surface than in boreholes on either side: the 'rise' is a result of the volcanic intrusions into the Carboniferous strata discussed later in this chapter. Old Red Sandstone has been found beneath Lambourn (and Sonning and Slough, to the north-east of the area covered in Figure 2.2). It is believed (Foster *et al.*, 1989) that the layer may continue beneath the whole of Berkshire, below the Carboniferous layers that have been found, and that, like those layers, been folded into a bowl by the Variscan orogeny.

Figure 2.3 is also my interpretation, this time of a large-scale, 2D map that was based on seismic scans. In that map the contour lines do not go 'all round'; in particular, the western corner is my guess at how they might join up. These scans go much deeper than the boreholes used to prepare Figure 2.2. I have included the major boreholes to make it easier to compare the two figures: the projection shows that the syncline may have been more than 1,200metres deep (more than 1,500metres below current Ordnance Survey datum (OSD: broadly, the present sea level). Please note that the vertical scale is about six times the horizontal scale.

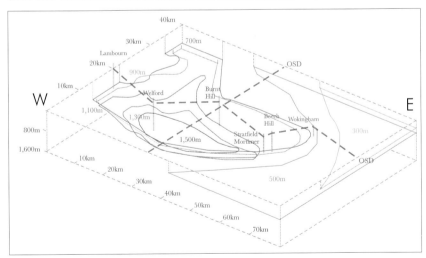

Figure 2.3: 3D projection of the Berkshire syncline
Redrawn by author from Foster *et al.*, 1989

Berkshire rocks laid down before the Cretaceous

Late in the Carboniferous period the Berkshire syncline filled with river-mouth sediments and a little coal (enough to justify digging the boreholes I am now taking advantage of, but not enough to justify mining). The 150 million years or so after the Carboniferous period are characterised by what is missing from the geological record. The word 'unconformity' appears frequently on BGS maps of the county. Borehole evidence from outside Berkshire suggests that 'the region was probably a rocky desert' during the 46 million years or so of the Permian period (Sumbler *et al.*, 1996). Now part of Pangæa, Britain was no longer under the sea, and had moved to between 20° and 25° north of the equator (the northern desert belt). No Permian strata remain in Berkshire. Triassic and Jurassic rocks, clays and sands have been found in boreholes, at depths varying from 200 to more than 1,000metres below the surface (62 to more than 850metres below the OSD). Gradually, over this period sediments washed off the London Platform by rivers turned Berkshire from low-lying land to submerged shoals. Fossilised coral reefs are found in Jurassic strata in Berkshire, as well as the well-known Oxford and Kimmeridge clays; *see Figure 2.4*. The sea seems to have advanced and retreated; at times the London Platform may have been under water. What is now the British Isles continued to move northwards.

Figure 2.4 shows where Jurassic (upper graph) and Triassic, Carboniferous and Devonian rock groups (lower graph) have been found in Berkshire, how thick they are and how far below the present surface. You will see that the boreholes at Burnt Hill, Stratfield Mortimer, Beech Hill and Slough found no Triassic layers below the Jurassic layers shown in the top panel: an unconformity representing around 90 million years' rocks, sands and clays that either were never laid down in these areas or have since eroded away. No boreholes found Permian layers between the Jurassic (or Triassic) and Carboniferous layers. Below Slough no Carboniferous layers were found, either; possibly 250 million years passed between when the Jurassic layers in the top panel, and the Devonian layer in the bottom panel, were laid down!

Both graphs follow a curved course halfway across the county, from the high ground in the north-west, to the lower ground south of Reading; then they give a snapshot of what lies below Slough. The upper graph continues on down into the lower one; the 'Younger' layer at the top is examined in Figures 3.1 and 4.1, *in Chapters 3 and 4.*

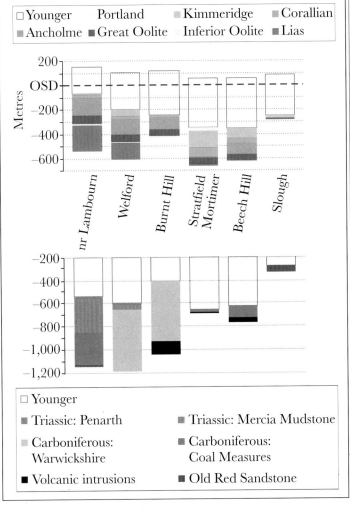

Figure 2.4: Jurassic and pre-Jurassic layers found in six bore-holes

Drawn by author from British Geological Survey data

If we follow the browny-grey band for the Great Oolite across the upper graph we can see the northern rim of the Berkshire syncline sweeping around what is still relatively high ground, then plunging nearly 200metres into the 'bowl' of the syncline, below what is now the valley of the Kennet. (The thin band of Great Oolite found under Slough is all that is left on the rim of the syncline.)

There are volcanic intrusions into Carboniferous layers at Burnt Hill, Stratfield Mortimer and Beech Hill. At Burnt Hill no (Carboniferous) Coal Measures layers have been found, and there are two thick layers of basalt with a narrow layer of tuff between them (tuff is essentially cooled, crystallised magmatic froth). The basalts are weathered, some at least of which took place in the open air (not under water). At Stratfield Mortimer and Beech Hill, the volcanic rocks are dolerite (similar to basalt, but coarser in texture) and form seams between Coal Measures layers. Dolerite cuts through the basalt in places at Burnt Hill. It is possible that we are seeing lava that has been erupted at Burnt Hill, but no structures suggesting a long-ago volcano have been found. The dolerite is clearly later and may be 'feeder' channels; it is also less weathered than the basalt. Another possibility, therefore, is that in all three places we are seeing volcanic rock that was intruded into gaps that happened to be in Carboniferous layers. Foster *et al.* (1989) believe that the mix of basalts and dolerites is comparable to igneous rocks laid down in Nottinghamshire and Leicestershire and observe that the dolerites cut through some beds of Westphalian age *(see Appendix 2)* but are overlain by others; so the volcanic events that produced these layers probably occurred during the Carboniferous.

Although no Jurassic or older rocks break the surface in Berkshire, readers in the west of the county do not have to travel far to see them. Near Abingdon, the Dry Sandford pits *(see Appendix 4 for directions)* contain fine exposures, as well as a fen (if you go in July, the marsh helleborines may be flowering). Visible at Dry Sandford are about 2.75metres of the Kingston **Formation**, below about 0.5metres of the Stanford Formation (and some much later soil and gravel) – my measuring rod is 1.75metres long. The Kingston Formation layers here are from the Beckley Sand member:

Photo 2.1: Jurassic Corallian sand and limestone, Dry Sandford pit

between layers of coarse sand are two beds of limestone named after the *Trigonia* clam shells, fossils of which can be found in them (but please do not go 'fossil hunting' without permission). The sands contain shell fragments and are stained a yellowish brown with limonite; they are 'cross-bedded' (i.e. have been laid down at different angles from the horizontal, as the tides or currents that carried them changed direction from time to time). The lower *Trigonia* bed (up to the first tick mark on the scale in Photo 2.1) was a pebbly beach containing fragments of coral that has been cemented together by calcium, possibly from dissolving shells: *see Photo 2.2.* The upper *Trigonia* bed (between the second and third tick marks on the scale) is made up of thin layers of shelly limestone, here and there separated by thin bands of clay. Above it is a thin band that has been called 'urchin marl' (a fine, sea-floor sediment containing occasional fossilised sea urchins), and above that lies the Stanford **Formation**, notably Coral 'rag' – the remains of a reef that covered much of Oxfordshire (between the top two tick marks on my scale).

Photo 2.2: Lower *Trigonia* bed at Dry Sandford pit, showing outlines of shells and coral fragments

Another interesting rock at Dry Sandford is a large sandstone 'dogger' at the edge of the fen *(see Photo 2.3)*: doggers are rounded bodies that have fully lithified (turned to stone) while otherwise identical surrounding material has not (in this case, Beckley sand like that seen *in Photos 2.1 and 2.2*).

Photo 2.3: Sandstone 'dogger' at Dry Sand-ford pit

3

The Cretaceous Period

BOUT 175 MILLION YEARS AGO (during the Jurassic period) the south Atlantic Ocean started to open, and Gondwana began to separate into South America, Africa, India, Antarctica and Australia. Gondwana and Laurasia (Laurentia and Asia) broke away from Pangæa. Africa moved northwards (closing the Tethys Ocean; what remains of it was dry for several million years before the Atlantic broke in to form the Mediterranean Sea). India separated from Africa and moved eastwards, eventually colliding with Asia.

The Cretaceous period began about 145 million years ago and lasted for about 84 million years. During this time the area that is now the UK moved to around 40° north of the equator. The north Atlantic began to open, splitting Laurasia: first it drove Greenland and Europe away from North America, then it separated Greenland from Europe. These movements pushed the London Platform, and with it Berkshire, above sea level. Sediments washed off the platform were laid down as the Wealden **group** in surrounding counties, particularly the Wessex Basin to the west, but none have been found beneath Berkshire. During the Aptian **age** the sea returned and first the Lower Greensand, then later the Selborne Group (Gault clays and the Upper Greensand), were laid down in deeper and deeper water. As the Cretaceous progressed, the sea continued to rise until most of Europe was covered, and for some 20 million years, starting in the Cenomanian age and continuing into the Campanian *(see Appendix 2)*, chalk was laid down *(see below)*. The Cretaceous ended with enormous volcanic eruptions in India (laying down the Deccan traps) and the impact of a large meteorite at Chicxulub in the Yucatàn, which led to mass extinctions all round the world; evidence of this K–Pg boundary is found at various sites in Berkshire.

Cretaceous rocks in Berkshire

As I mentioned, no Wealden Group rocks have been found beneath Berkshire (although they have been found as close as Kingsclere and Shalford); after the Jurassic there is a gap of perhaps 30 to 40 million years in the geological record, supporting the view that Berkshire was above sea level during this period. (The Wealden Group is mostly silts, clays, muds and sands, interpreted as river-borne sediment. You might expect to find such sediment 'fanning out' from a river mouth into the sea so covering a wide area, but further inland it would be confined to river channels so cover a narrow area, or to the bottoms of lakes and lagoons so be plentiful in some places and absent elsewhere.)

By contrast, Lower Greensand layers are found in most of the boreholes that penetrate that deeply. These are mainly sands and sandstones (with some silt and clay) so, like the Wealden Group, are believed to be river-borne detritus (Sumbler *et al.*, 1996); but because the Lower Greensand is present in Berkshire (unlike Wealden Group rocks) this suggests that by the time it was being laid down the sea had risen to cover the county. Moreover, Selborne Group and Grey and White Chalk layers (which are sediments laid down in increasingly deep seas) are found over most of Berkshire. This indicates that the county was beneath a rising sea during the second half of the period.

Cretaceous beds were found in 94% of the boreholes for which I collated BGS data *(see Chapter 1)*, and the following summary might interest some readers:

Layers:	White Chalk beds	Grey Chalk beds	Selborne Group beds	Lower Greensand beds	*All Cretaceous:*
Mainly:	Chalk with flints; some chalk rock	Clayey chalk without flints; can include limestone	Upper Greensand (can include sandstone) and Gault clays	Sands, sandstones and some clays	
Found in:	93%*	91%†	NA	NA	94%*
Thickest bed:	246 metres	104 metres	126 metres	58 metres	354 metres
Narrowest bed:	18 metres	8 metres	50 metres	6 metres	32 metres
Median thickness:	81 metres	69 metres	89 metres	16 metres	120 metres
Notes:	* Of 492 boreholes.				
	† Of the 68 boreholes that went below the White Chalk.				

Please note that for the three bottom rows of this table I only included layers if the borehole penetrated to the layer below; in other words, I only took into account layers for which we know the total thickness. I have not supplied percentages for beds below the Grey Chalk because only 38 of the boreholes went that deep.

As this table shows, the thickness of these layers can vary widely. Another feature that varies widely is how near the surface they are (i.e. how thick younger, higher layers may be):

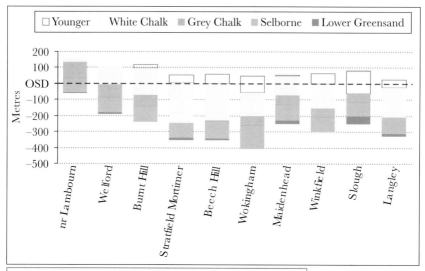

Figure 3.1: Cretaceous layers found in ten boreholes

Drawn by author from British Geological Survey data

Figure 3.1 follows a zig-zag course across the county, from the high ground in the north-west, to the lower ground south of Reading and then along the Thames. It's a little fanciful (but not ridiculous) to trace the outline of the Berkshire syncline as far as Wokingham, after which this flight of fancy breaks down, as we're talking of the London Basin; and we can observe how the White Chalk thins over the high ground. Nothing should be read into the apparent absence of Grey Chalk at Stratfield Mortimer and Langley; the Stratfield Mortimer borehole was drilled to look for oil, and the drillers were chiefly interested in much older layers, while the logs for the Langley borehole suggest that Grey Chalk was present but are too cursory for me to be certain where it began.

The Lower Cretaceous

The period is divided into a Lower and an Upper period (each with six ages – *see Appendix 2*). The Lower Cretaceous is well represented in southern England, but not especially well in Berkshire: the

Hastings Beds (mostly sandstones) are up to 400metres thick over parts of the Kent and Sussex Wealds, but absent here; I have already mentioned the absence of the (later) Wealden Group; the Woburn Sands formation of the Lower Greensand Group (also mostly sandstones) is found here and there, but is nowhere very thick.

The Selborne Group spans the boundary between the Lower and Upper Cretaceous. In Berkshire it is fairly widespread, in fairly thick layers (as Figure 3.1 suggests). The Gault formation is mostly stiff blue clay that was laid down in fairly deep water during the Albian age (between about 94Ma and 101Ma – Ma = millions of years before the present). Above it we find the Upper Greensand formation (fine-grained sand and sandstone, sometimes stained a bluey-green by glauconite, a potassium iron aluminosilicate mica that forms in shallow water under reducing conditions: (K, Na) $(Fe^{3+}, Al, Mg)_2(Si, Al)_4O_{10}(OH)_2))$. The Upper Greensand was laid down from late in the Albian age until the Cenomanian age (which ran from about 90Ma). It is not always possible to match geological strata to named ages and dates; boundaries between ages may be defined by fossil groups, not types of rock, and sedimentary rocks may have continued to be laid down in one part of their range long after they ceased to be laid down in another part.

The oldest layer that is visible at the surface in Berkshire is the (Selborne) Upper Greensand, and we can see it along a short stretch at the top of a bridleway called Bungum Lane, just outside Inkpen *(for directions, see Appendix 4)*. It is most obvious in the form of sandstone cobbles containing pebbles and fossilised shells.

The Cretaceous was named after the chalk that was laid down through the Upper part of the period.

Chalk and flint

Chalk is a very fine-grained limestone, formed under water mostly from the skeletons (tests) of relatively deep-sea (pelagic) algæ called coccolithophorids (unicellular phytoplankton). Interestingly, chalk only forms within a band in the sea. If the water is too shallow, although coccolithophorids may be present, they are not in great numbers so their tests form merely part of the sands, pebbles, river silts, decomposing seaweeds and other elements building up on the sea-floor. If it is too deep (at or below the carbonate compensation depth, CCD), the cold and pressure cause dissolved carbon dioxide (CO_2) to react with the calcium carbonate ($CaCO_3$) in the tests to leave calcium and 'bicarbonate' (HCO_3), both of which dissolve in water. CCD depends on temperature, pressure and the

Photo 3.1: Upper Greensand cobbles, Bungum Lane

amount of carbon dioxide dissolved in the seawater, but currently is between 4,200metres and 5,000metres down; it is believed to have been much nearer the surface during the Cretaceous period because volcanic activity meant that, although the oceans were warmer, there was much more carbon dioxide both in the air and in the oceans.

It has been estimated that chalk was laid down at a rate of between 1 and 2cm per 1,000 years (Toghill, 2000, p. 145). Much of it is minute crystals of calcite (chalk 'flour') that, under pressure, have splintered from the coccoliths, rotated and locked together. Unlike most limestone there is little or no chemical cement binding these crystals together, except where chalk rock has formed, which happens after unusually high pressure and/or heat has caused calcium carbonate and/or organic debris to precipitate as calcite cement, filling gaps between grains.

Occasionally, complete coccoliths are found, and other micro- or nanofossils, and in some areas the shells of bivalves form beds in the chalk. These are usually broken; it is rare to find a complete fossil (both shells, found close enough together to recognise that they were part of the same animal or, if you are lucky, still joined as they would have been in life).

Flint, a variety of (the normally pelagic) chert, seems to have formed between 97 and 65 million years ago within gaps in the chalk left by fossils, burrows, 'other organic structures' and joints and cracks. It consists of quartz and opaline silica, two different crystal forms of silicon dioxide, SiO_2. Opaline silica is a stage prior to crystallisation, in which the silicon dioxide forms small spheres; when it crystallises as quartz, the crystals are usually six-sided columns ending in hexagonal pyramids. Flints can crystallise around siliceous tests (similar to the shell or exoskeleton) of radiolaria (unicellular zooplankton) and other siliceous material, such as the spicules of some sponges. Occasionally, moulds of complete creatures turn up, where the void left by the decayed body has been entirely filled with flint. There is some debate about where the silicon dioxide that formed the flint came from, especially since giant, 'paramoudra' flints can be the size of a human being, but one suggestion is that it represents local concentrations of the remains of siliceous plants or animals. It is believed that these remains dissolved in alkaline sea-floor ooze, which flowed into gaps; organic matter, decomposing, gave off hydrogen sulphide (H_2S) which oxidised and turned its surroundings acidic, causing the silicon dioxide to precipitate as opaline silica, filling the gaps. As mud, silt and tests continued to build up on the sea floor earlier layers were gradually buried deeper and deeper. With increasing depth heat and pressure changed the opaline silica to microcrystalline quartz.

Flints are found in the higher layers of what used to be called the Middle chalk and the Upper chalk. These divisions are problematic: one traditional subdivision is between grey chalk (below) and white chalk (above); another is between lower, middle and upper sequences, but these do not quite map either on to the grey/white division, or on to the accepted 'ages' within the Cretaceous period *(see Appendix 2)*. Recently, more detailed subdivisions have been accepted by the BGS; these various systems can be reconciled as follows:

Age (Ma):	Traditional nomenclature:			Current (southern England):	
~82	WHITE	UPPER	Top rock/ Chalk rock	Portsdown formation	
				Culver formation	Spetisbury **member**
					Tarrant member
				Margate member	Newhaven formation
~85.8				Seaford formation	
		MIDDLE	Spurious chalk rock	Lewes Nodular formation	
				New Pit formation	
~93.5			Melbourn rock	Holywell Nodular formation	
			Plenus **marls**		
	GREY	LOWER	Grey rock	Zig Zag formation	
			Chalk marl	West Melbury marl formation	
			Glauconitic marl		
~100	UPPER GREENSAND OR GAULT CLAY				
NOTE:	Southern England system in Rawson *et al.* (2001).				

In Berkshire, the beds of White Chalk tend to be shallower than those further west (Wiltshire) or north-east (the Chilterns), and they tend to contain layers of chalk rock. This has been called the Berkshire–Chilterns shelf. Some sequences are absent from much of the county or have been eroded away – the layers above the Margate member, in most places the Seaford formation *(but see Photo 3.2)*, much of the Lewes and New Pit formations, the marly layers of the Zig Zag and West Melbury formations *(see Photo 3.3)*.

Photo 3.2: Cookham Dean: Seaford chalk; note bedding and layers of both tabular and nodular flint

This erosion contributed to the clay-with-flints that covers much of the Berkshire Downs. As chalk dissolved in water, flints were left behind, and often they show no sign of stream or river 'rounding'. Insoluble material left over from the weathered chalk and other eroded rocks collected round the flints,

Photo 3.3: Near Inkpen: West Melbury chalk; note bedding, vertical fractures and absence of marl

to form a range of (often sandy) clays.

Water

Edmunds *et al.* (1987) describe 'the Chalk [as] the most important **aquifer** in England'. Some of this is Cretaceous sea water that has remained trapped above the Gault clay of the Selborne Group, but most is rain that has fallen on the Berkshire Downs and the Chilterns to the north, Salisbury Plain to the west and the North Downs to the south and east.

Mean annual rainfall in Berkshire is about 750mm per annum, but according to Stephen Burt of the Royal Meteorological Society 'average annual rainfall in central Reading is around 650mm: over the western downlands around half as much again falls (around 900–950mm) in an average year, while the drier east of the county averages less than 600mm… in 1921 only 327mm fell at Bisham Vicarage, the lowest annual total on record for Berkshire, while in 1903 1,204mm fell at Farnborough Rectory (in the north-west)'. Moreover, 'snow falls on 10–15 days in a normal year in most parts of Berkshire, increasing to 20 days or more on the western hills'.

To reach the aquifer, around 40% of this water flows through holes and cracks in the chalk; these are more common in valleys than on ridges, and more common in the upper 60metres of the chalk, which explains some of the concentration of deeper boreholes – *see Figure 1.1*. Chalk is highly porous, whether or not cracks open in it.

Chalk ridges tend to be of the *cuesta* type *(see Figure 3.2)*: a steep scarp face on one side cutting through sloping strata and a gentle dip on the other (often matching the dip of the strata). Springs are common on the scarp face, where water may flow out around bands of flint, chalk rock, the Melbourn Rock at the base of the White Chalk, the Chilton Stone within the Grey Chalk or out of the junction between the Grey Chalk and the Upper Greensand (Selborne Group). They are rare on the dip slope, which is usually drained by a few major streams that are fed more by seepage

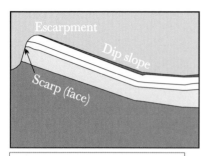

Figure 3.2: Typical chalk ridge form

Redrawn by author from *Oxford Dictionary of Geology and Earth Sciences*

than by springs. Sections may be dry for some or much of the year, reviving after the autumn rains. These are known as winterbournes – 'bourne', a stream, can be traced back, via the Scottish 'burn', to various old Germanic languages. In some cases a winterbourne is reactivated by springs: Photos 3.4 and 3.5 show a source of the River Lambourn that is fed by springs (*see particularly Photo 3.5*; to find Lynch Wood, *see Appendix 4*).

Photo 3.4: Lynch Wood winterbourne, Lambourn

Other examples can be found further along the Lambourn, on tributaries of the Kennet, on the Pang, the Enborne and the Loddon, and many brooks are winterbournes for much of their course.

The speed and power with which chalk rivers and streams flow are generally too low to move stones and gravel, in part because

Photo 3.5: Lynch Wood winterbourne; note columns of ripples from springs

the course is rarely steep and in part because water can seep through chalk even where there are no cracks or holes. This has six consequences:

◊ the channel winds about (straight sections are usually man-made)
◊ it is usually shallow (on average, a stream's width is 33 times its depth)
◊ except where it meets impermeable soils (e.g. clays), there is little branching
◊ riffles and pools tend to be small and close together *(see below)*
◊ gravel shoals are infrequent (which is not the same as saying that gravel is rare in the bed) and
◊ whatever the stream or river has cut through can often be clearly seen in the banks or bed.

Streams with sand or gravel beds often alternate between deep sections (pools) and shallow ones (riffles). In winding streams pools are often found on bends and riffles between bends; and shoals can form on the inside of bends where the water flows less quickly. However, because chalk streams are shallow and flow with less power than streams in steeper country or over less permeable material, they only move stones or gravel during occasional storm floods, which means the bed is not scoured deeper by stones passing over it as in other streams. Even sand and silt are only moved short distances before the water can no longer carry them. But chalk does eventually dissolve in water, meaning that much of the sand, gravel, clay and silt in chalk streams is left over after the surrounding chalk (and some other constituents) has been dissolved (chemical erosion), rather than being carried down the channel from the headwaters (frictional erosion).

The K–Pg boundary

Around 67 million years ago the Indian tectonic plate began to move rapidly northwards, away from the African plate. Over the next 4 million years a vast series of volcanic eruptions covered the Western Ghats, the mountain range that runs parallel to the western coast of India, in successive layers of lava that have become known as the Deccan Traps ('traps' after the Swedish word for stairs). The Traps may have covered an area nearly half the size of present-day India; even after erosion and continuing tectonic movements around $500,000km^2$ of lava flows can still be seen. Worldwide temperatures are believed to have dropped about 2°C during this period, thanks to gases emitted in these eruptions.

Shortly after this (in geological terms), about 66 million years ago, an asteroid or comet struck the Earth, in deep water off the shore of the Yucatàn peninsula. This was near the present-day town of Chicxulub, after which the crater has been named. Estimates of the object's diameter range from 11 to 81km; the crater is 150km in diameter and 20km deep (and may originally have been 10km deeper). Shockwaves triggered major earthquakes around the world. Some think that the impact increased the permeability of the Indian plate, allowing much more magma (and the accompanying gases) to reach the surface and form the Deccan Traps; 'peak flow' in the Deccan seems to have followed the Chicxulub impact. A dust cloud may have covered the entire planet for up to ten years, blocking most or all sunlight; this would have been exacerbated by the vapourising of carbonate and sulfate rocks in the impact, hugely increasing atmospheric carbon dioxide and sulfate aerosols (particles so small they can hang in the atmosphere). In the upper atmosphere such aerosols can have a cooling effect by absorbing, reflecting or scattering solar radiation, while in the lower atmosphere they provide nuclei around which water vapour collects to form drops, which dissolve the sulfates, increasing the acidity of the rain that eventually falls. Acid rain kills plants, but when it falls on the sea in sufficient quantities to increase the water's acidity it has an equally lethal effect on much sea life.

Other, smaller craters of a similar age have been found, between latitudes 20° and 70° North, but the 'multiple impact' hypothesis remains controversial. Likewise controversial is the question how far mass extinction was 'already under way', or 'encouraged', or 'caused' by the Deccan eruptions and the Chicxulub meteorite. What is not disputed is the scale of the mass extinction that followed. About 17% of all families, 50% of all genera and 75% of all species became extinct, including the ammonites and the dinosaurs (apart from those that became birds).

Around the world, a thin layer of clay is found at the boundary of the Cretaceous and Palæogene strata containing iridium; the concentration can reach 6 parts per billion by weight, which is a great deal more than the amounts usually found on Earth (average 0.4 parts per billion). Meteorites often contain large quantities of iridium, and higher-than-usual concentrations of the metal have been found around other known meteorite craters. It is believed that the Chicxulub asteroid may have contained iridium that was vapourised by the impact and carried into the atmosphere with the other impact material, and that this gradually settled out with the rest of the dust cloud. The layer was first named by German geologists (the boundary between the *Kreidezeit* – Cretaceous period – and the Palæogene – *see Appendix 2*) and the K has been retained to avoid confusion with the Carboniferous period. It can clearly be seen at Owl Pit, near Stanford Dingley *(see Appendix 4 for directions, and Photo 3.6)*, as a thin, dark band between the White Chalk and the reddish Upnor Formation sands.

Photo 3.6: Owl Pit, near Stanford Dingley: the K–Pg boundary

4

The Palæogene and Neogene Periods

TARTING IN THE PRESENT, CENOZOIC ERA, about 66 million years ago, two sets of tectonic events raised the UK above sea level and formed the present geography. There were major volcanic events in northern and western Britain, and plate collisions that drove up an almost continuous chain of mountains from the Alps to the Himalayas caused folding and faulting in much of southern Britain. What is now the UK continued to drift northwards, to its current position about 50° north of the equator, and it was also pushed eastwards by the spreading of the Atlantic Ocean. The volcanic activity had ceased by the Eocene (about 55 million years ago) and has left little evidence in Berkshire (and that evidence debatable: *see Chapter 2*). The Alpine orogeny (mountain building) has not yet ended; by possibly about 35 million years ago it had interacted with the spreading of the Atlantic to fold the London Platform into a London Basin, the slopes of which are relatively gentle to the west (in the Berkshire Downs) but steep further east – parts of the Hog's Back dip at 55°. Faults dating back to the Variscan orogeny (*see Chapter 2*) probably contributed to the steepness.

The climate warmed during the Palæocene (the first part of the Palæogene period) and rainfall was plentiful but probably seasonal. The sea did not rise or fall much but water-driven erosion and the action of rivers caused coastlines to advance and retreat across Berkshire several times.

A basin and a pericline

The London Basin runs from east and south of Reading north-eastwards into the North Sea, following folds in Mesozoic rocks that have been inferred from gravitational analysis. Reading and Slough are on the northern rim of the basin, which lies beneath north-western Surrey, most of Greater London and Essex, and south-east Suffolk. The Windsor **pericline** may have been thrust up as part of the folding and movement that saw the London Platform inverted to become the massive synform that we see today[*] – the timing is consistent with this and the pericline is oriented roughly west–east, which is also consistent.

A pericline is a concentric fold; where convex (as at Windsor) there is typically a core of older rocks surrounded with later layers. The Windsor pericline is a type known as a dome and Figure 4.1 shows why.

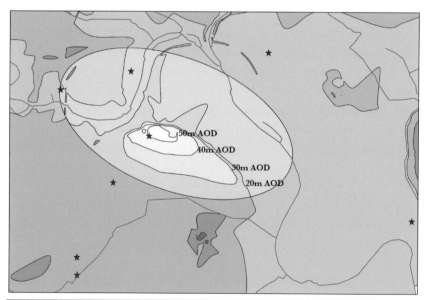

Figure 4.1: The Windsor pericline

Extracted by author from map at Figure 1.1; Ordnance Survey and British Geological Survey data used to draw the map

An area extending west and north from the northern part of

[*]   The London Basin may not be a syncline, perhaps because it is not a bowl but a massive groove that runs out into the North Sea. I am not geologist enough to be sure of this.

Windsor Great Park is an inlier: an area of White Chalk surrounded by much younger Thames Group and Lambeth Group beds. A little below the centre an imposing lump of chalk rises 35metres, piercing the younger beds that surround it, and on top of this Windsor Castle was built. (In the ellipse the yellow areas show where White Chalk has pierced the surface.) This is not a survivor, left behind when chalk all round it was eroded away, but a fold pushed up during the late Eocene or Oligocene periods *(see Appendix 2)* by a northwards-directed thrust. It is possible that older layers were pushed up at the same time, but none of the boreholes marked on Figure 4.1 (by stars) goes deep enough to establish this.

Palæogene rocks in Berkshire

The Lambeth Group (which includes the Reading formation), the Thames Group (which includes the London clay) and the Bracklesham Group (which includes the Bagshot formation) were laid down while Berkshire was gradually being pushed upwards between about 60 and about 44 million years ago (late Palæocene, early to mid-Eocene). Virtually nothing survives from the Oligocene, Miocene and most of the Pliocene **epochs**, however, so perhaps I should have left Neogene out of this chapter's title. Presumably, the county had risen above sea level by the Oligocene (so sediments, if any, would have been carried in by wind or along rivers).

For comparison, Figure 4.2 includes data from the ten boreholes illustrated *in Figure 3.1 above* (in two of which, Lambourn and Welford, there is nothing above the White Chalk) plus another seven, most included to show how the Palæogene layers vary, both in thickness and in the rocks, clays and sands that make them up (Eastbury was included because its position was helpful in preparing Figure 2.1). Eleven boreholes recorded younger layers that are not shown above; it is quite possible that the other six contained *something* above the Palæogene layers, even if only a few centimetres of soil and even if the drillers' log apparently suggests otherwise. Almost all these boreholes were dug or drilled with the aim of finding water, oil or coal a long way below the surface and the logs of many show little or no interest in the 'head', 'drift', 'ballast' or other materials at the top.

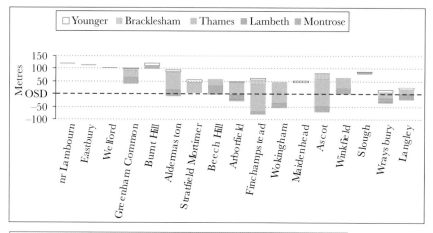

Figure 4.2: Palæogene layers found in seventeen boreholes
Drawn by author from British Geological Survey data

Palæogene beds were found in 65% of the 492 boreholes for which I collated BGS data *(see Chapter 1)*, and the following summary might interest some readers:

Layers:	Barton Group beds	Brackle-sham Group beds	Thames Group beds	Lambeth Group beds	Mon-trose Group beds	*All Palæo-gene:*
Mainly:	Barton clay	Cam-berley and Bagshot sands	London clay	Wool-wich, Reading and Upnor sands, silts and clays	Thanet sands	
Found in:	<1%	9%	44%	62%	1%	65%

Layers:	Barton Group beds	Brackle- sham Group beds	Thames Group beds	Lambeth Group beds	Mon- trose Group beds	*All Palæo- gene:*
Thickest bed:	30 metres	81 metres	114 metres	40 metres	9 metres	184 metres
Narrow- est bed:	NA	1.5 metres	2 metres	1 metre	1 metre	1 metre
Median thickness:	NA	10 metres	28 metres	21 metres	5 metres	31 metres

Please note that for the three bottom rows of this table I only included layers if the borehole penetrated to the layer below; in other words, I only took into account layers for which we know the total thickness.

Only one borehole claimed a Barton Group bed, and the Group is normally found some way south of Berkshire, so it is arguable that I should have left this out. As this table shows, Bracklesham Group beds are not found very often in Berkshire, and Montrose Group beds are rarer still. The table might give the impression that Palæogene beds in Berkshire are often very narrow, but only some are: while 15% of the boreholes included in the table found 10metres or less of Palæogene beds, 30% of them found more than 50metres of Palæogene beds. Conversely, two boreholes near Maidenhead found Palæogene beds (of the Lambeth group) that were only 1metre thick; neither is shown in Figure 4.2.

As with the chalk *(see Chapter 3)* the divisions accepted by the BGS have changed over time, which can make it difficult to 'place' the names given in borehole logs within the current system:

Age (Ma):	Traditional nomenclature:		Current nomenclature: (if in brackets, presence in Berkshire is uncertain)		
~34	Barton clay		(Barton group)	(Barton clay formation)	
~41	Upper Bagshot sands	Barton beds	Brackle-sham group	Camberley sand formation	
					(Stanners Hill pebble beds)
	Middle Bagshot sands	Brackle-sham beds		(Windlesham formation)	
	Lower Bagshot sands	Bagshot beds		Bagshot formation	Swinley clay member
~48	London clay		Thames group	London clay formation	Claygate member
					(Aveley member)
	London clay basement beds			Harwich formation	
~56	Woolwich and Reading beds		Lambeth group	(Woolwich formation)	
				Reading formation	Upper mottled beds
					Lower mottled beds
				Upnor formation	
~59	Thanet sands		Montrose group	Thanet formation	
~66	CRETACEOUS PERIOD				
NOTE:	Extracted and organised by me from Aldiss (2012).				

In this table, treat the 'Age' column with caution; many of these types of sediment were being laid down at the same time in different places. For example, a borehole near Stanford Dingley found Woolwich formation beds below Reading Formation beds.

Clay, iron and water

Clays have been mentioned several times already, but they are particularly important in this chapter and Chapter 5 so this is a good point to discuss them. The word describes very fine mineral particles (hydrous aluminium phyllosilicates, or aluminium and silicon ions bonded into minute plates by oxygen and hydroxyl ions). To be 'clay' most of the particles must be less in diameter than a figure that different groups of scientists disagree over – chemists say 0.001mm, geologists 0.002mm and soil scientists 0.0039mm. Silt is made of slightly larger particles: up to 0.062mm in diameter.

There are three main 'families' of clay minerals – kaolinites ($Al_2Si_2O_5(OH)_4$), smectites ((Na^+, Ca^{2+})$_3 \cdot nH_2O$ [($Al_{1.5}Fe^{3+}_{0.2}Mg_{0.3}$) $Si_4O_{10}(OH)_2$]) and illites ((K, H_3O)(Al, Mg, Fe)$_2$(Si, Al)$_4O_{10}[(OH)_2 \cdot (H_2O)]$]) – and some other minerals are sometimes classed as clay minerals – chlorite (ClO_2) is one. Clays tend to swell when they take up water and shrink when they dry: the flat profile of the particles means that water sticks to them (water has very high surface tension), and this means that relatively little passes through. It also means that water can run along a buried clay layer until it finds somewhere to emerge, as a spring or a stream: Photo 4.1 shows an example of such a spring washing iron from the gravels above into a stream below. Smectites swell and shrink more than the other two types of clay.

Most clays form through chemical weathering of rocks. Rocks containing feldspars (such as granites) can produce kaolinites when exposed to *acid* weathering (for example, because rainwater might contain acids from dissolved carbon dioxide), or illites when exposed to *alkaline* weathering (for example, when the acids in rainwater have been consumed, calcium bicarbonate can be left behind). Igneous deposits exposed to alkaline weathering can produce smectites, but smectites are also left behind after chalk is dissolved and after chemical weathering of glauconite. Chlorite is another product of chemical weathering of igneous deposits.

Chemical weathering can take place in the open air, but it can also be a side-effect of hydro-thermal processes, movement of heat and water that takes place under-ground, under pressure. The 'water' might not be liquid, but rather chemical reactions involving hydrogen and oxygen.

Across Berkshire but more often in the east of the county we find 'red streams', coloured by ochre (hydrated ferric oxide, $Fe_2H_2O_4$) in a circular process. Ferric oxide (rust, Fe_2O_3) is washed out of gravels or sands by rain; normally it remains as small, insoluble particles which are simply suspended and carried in water. However, there are two ways in which it becomes (partly) soluble. In soils, humic acids (decomposed organic remains) can bind to the iron, giving (partly soluble) iron humates. Bogs typically lack oxygen, and capture some from suspended ferric oxides, leaving soluble ferrous salts. In suspension or in solution the iron is carried by water until a clay layer is reached, along which it might run until it emerges as a spring *(see Photo 4.1)* or a stream, or where it

Photo 4.1: Spring emerging between Silchester terrace gravels and London clay, Bow-down Woods

might pool to create a bog.

While being carried by streams, ferrous salts or iron humates can be exposed to oxygen again and simply oxidise; or a variety of bacteria can cause them to oxidise. This ferric oxide can become hydrated as it is carried or simply be deposited; in pools and bogs thick layers of ochre and ferric oxide can build up, promoting the presence of iron bacteria.

Montrose Group

A Montrose Group formation (Thanet sands) has been found, usually around 70metres below the present surface (thus about 20metres below present sea level), in a triangle around Binfield and Arborfield, south and east of Reading, and in two boreholes south of Windsor. As the name suggests, this is about the furthest west that these layers are found. Flints at the base of the layer are often stained blue or green by glauconite, and lower layers (which can contain more silt and clay than sand) are fine-grained, suggesting that the first Thanet formation layers were probably laid down as seabed sediments. On present-day beaches, finer particles are deposited offshore, coarser ones (sand and pebbles) closer inshore; since more recent Thanet sands (i.e. higher beds) are coarser, this suggests that the coastline was moving (since sea level is not believed to have risen significantly during this period). The beds are pale grey to brownish grey when freshly exposed, but weather to a pale yellow-grey.

Lambeth Group

As the tables above suggest, beds from three different formations in this group can be found beneath much of Berkshire. Both 'Lambeth' and 'Woolwich and Reading Beds' – before 1995, the name for the whole Lambeth Group – frequently appear in borehole records.

Late in the Palæocene epoch, while Berkshire was still under water, the Upnor formation was laid down. This is mostly sand; the lower levels are often heavily stained by glauconite and can contain narrow bands of flint or clay (also usually stained); the upper levels are usually pale; weathering bleaches all levels. Sometimes grains of glauconite can be seen in it: a 'pepper and salt' appearance has been reported. Only two boreholes reported Upnor sands, though they can be seen in the Owl (chalk) Pit near Stanford Dingley *(see Photos 3.6, 5.1 and 5.2 and Appendix 4)* where the sand is heavily weathered and the glauconite in it has broken down to goethite ($\alpha\cdot Fe^{3+}O(OH)$) or limonite ($Fe^{3+}O(OH)\cdot nH_2O$) (red-brown or yellow-brown). Sometimes, where calcium carbonate and pyrite ($Fe^{2+}S_2$) are found together, the pyrite oxidises to produce sulphuric acid (H_2SO_4), which reacts with the calcium carbonate to produce gypsum. The sands can be fine or coarse (though Upnor sands are usually coarser than the Thanet sand), and this along with the occasional presence of clay and the fact that the flints found in the formation are usually well rounded suggests a coastal, or possibly river-mouth deposit.

The Reading formation is mainly multicoloured clay but can contain sand in the lower parts of a deposit, or in channels suggesting river channels. It is believed to have been laid down in lagoons and/or mudflats spread across a wide, level plain. It is found across the whole county (unless, as on some ridge-tops and notably along the course of the Thames, everything above the chalk has been eroded away). Where there is no London clay present *(see 'Thames Group', below)* sometimes only Quaternary layers are found above the Reading formation, which makes it all the more surprising that the only outcrop that the public may still visit is at the Pincent's Kiln Site of Special Scientific Interest *(see Appendix 4 for directions)*. Sadly *(see Photos 4.2 and 4.3)* this is in lamentable condition. If not busy, Specialised Paintwork may be prepared to open their gate so you can see more of it. This SSSI is the remains of a clay pit (Reading beds have been extensively mined to make bricks since the Roman period), and the colour has mostly weathered out of the face that is still visible. Look hard, as fossils of shark's teeth and Palæocene plants can be found.

The clays may be red (stained with iron, typically hæmatite Fe_2O_3) though brown (ditto, typically pyrite) and blue (glauconitic) beds occur in the Reading formation. Hæmatite can form 'rosettes' in voids in the formation, and (occasionally) iron nodules have formed in the

Photo 4.2:
Pincent's Kiln
SSSI

clay. More often, calcium carbonate forms rosettes or nodules, and these nodules have been described as rocks (even limestone); but they are not, really. The BGS divide the formation into a Lower Mottled Clay and an Upper Mottled Clay, but admit that the boundary can be hard to identify; occasionally the layers are separated by a thin grey, blue or black layer of clay (as was found, for example, in excavations for the A34 Newbury bypass). The BGS report on the Lambeth Group states that the Woolwich formation is only found east of Berkshire, so perhaps the bore-holes that logged it at Stanford Dingley and Jack's Booth actually found Reading formation beds. (The Stanford Dingley borehole found 4.2metres of Woolwich formation sand below 16.3metres of Reading formation clay: 20.7 metres would be fairly thick for the Reading formation, particularly at this point on a fairly steep scarp slope, but possible. This kind of interbedding is common in London but would be unusual as far

Photo 4.3:
Pincent's Kiln SSSI:
Reading Formation
clay (and some
sand)

west as Stanford Dingley.) The Woolwich formation is typically thin, interleaved layers of grey to grey-brown fine sand, silt and clay, and often contains thick bands of shells, oysters, other bivalves or a range of gastropods. All of this is consistent with a river-mouth, or possibly lake-bed deposit.

Occasionally gypsum can form in Woolwich beds, as described for the Upnor formation above.

Smectite is dominant in Lambeth Group clays to the east of Berkshire, but there can be significant local variation: illite and kaolinite are more dominant in Lambeth Group clays in Hampshire, for example, and a borehole near Newbury found bands of smectite alternating with bands of illite or kaolinite (Entwisle *et al.*, 2013). Entwisle and colleagues also speculated that ash from volcanic activity around Greenland or the Faroes could lie behind smectite 'peaks' in some Upnor and Woolwich Formation layers.

Sarsen stones

Late in the period when the Upnor formation was being laid down, some concretions of sand, sometimes including flint gravels, would gradually harden during repeated wet and dry cycles to form sarsens. We know that this is how they formed because similar rocks form today in a similar way, often in desert areas: they are called silcretes (concretions cemented together with silica). As water evaporates from the ground surface, sub-surface water is drawn upwards and, where this contains silica, it cements sand grains together.

Sarsens continued to form during the period of the Reading Formation; in the west of the county they are often found on ridge tops, where no layers survive above the chalk and they may be all that survives of sandy Palæogene beds. This suggests that northern and western Berkshire may have been a floodplain, generally dry but prone to occasional serious floods. Photos 4.4, 5 and 6 show a collection of sarsens: note holes left after tree roots rotted away, casts of roots and branches, ripple marks and, in Photo 4.6's close-up of the broken sarsen in Photo 4.4, the fineness of the grains that have been cemented together and how far the iron staining has penetrated. *See also Photo 7.2.*

Photo 4.4: Sarsens at Chapel Farm, Leckhampstead

Photo 4.5: Close-up of sarsen, showing casts of ancient roots and branches and ripple marks	Photo 4.6: Close-up of sarsen, showing depth of weathering

Thames Group

The Thames Group in Berkshire generally means the London clay; one borehole records the Harwich Formation (at the bottom of the Group) and five boreholes record the Claygate member (at the top of it).

The Stanford Dingley borehole mentioned *in the section on the Lambeth Group* found 7metres of Harwich formation sands and gravels between Reading beds and London clay. This may be the same as what is elsewhere recorded as 'London clay basement beds', so the Harwich formation may appear elsewhere in Berkshire. That said, the formation was given a formal identity largely to address features found in Essex (as the name suggests), so this question may be academic.

The Thames Group was laid down throughout the Eocene, so it may lie over Bracklesham Group beds *(described below)* and later Lambeth Group beds may lie over London clay. This is sometimes described as 'interleaving'. While fewer boreholes found London clay than found Reading beds, the geographical spread is just as wide; though (predictably) while most boreholes in the east of the county found London clay, west of about Thatcham records are more sparse and the average thickness reduces further west. Like the Reading beds, London clay tends to be thinner on ridge-tops – or even absent from them – and the same is true along both the Thames and the Kennet, which have sometimes cut through to the Reading beds – in places the Thames might have cut through to the chalk. The thickness of the beds can vary quite markedly over short distances: for example 59metres of London clay was found at Newbury and Crookham Golf Club and 24metres less than a mile away at Greenham Common, while at Woolhampton 55metres were found on the ridge above the village but only 3metres at the public well in the village, less than half a mile away and down in the Kennet valley.

The clay was laid down in relatively deep water. It is usually blue-grey or a grey-brown, and weathers to brown and grey. The clay usually contains silt and can contain thin beds of sand, shells, rounded flints or even 'cementstones', remains of old reefs cemented together into a form of limestone by calcium carbonate. It is often bioturbated (prone to root holes, burrows and other marks left by long-dead animals and plants). It has been divided into five different members, of which only one has been recorded in Berkshire (though another, the Aveley member, was found at Staines so may extend into the county). Smectite, illite and kaolinite *(see above)* are all present, along with some chlorite; there is between one-fifth and one-third quartz; the clay can also contain feldspar and gypsum, and pyrite, and the sulphuric acid all of these give off in oxidation can attack limestone-based cements (e.g. Portland) and concretes. There is believed to be more smectite present than dissolution of chalk would have provided;

weathering of glauconite in the Upper Greensand may have contributed; weathering of volcanic ash deposits has also been suggested (Entwisle *et al.*, 2013 – though this is outside the period they studied; Kemp and Wagner, 2006).

The Claygate member tends to be a darker grey, more sandy than most London clay and can contain concretions of broken stones, rounded pebbles, etc. cemented together in a heavily iron-bearing matrix. Some of these are known as septarian nodules: rough spheroids made up of blocks cemented together in a radial pattern. Claygate sand is finer than the typical Bagshot sand *(see next section)*.

Bracklesham Group

Matching formations in this group to borehole records is less straightforward even than for the previous groups. 'Bagshot beds' are found relatively widely *(see below)*, and eight boreholes between Crowthorne and Ascot record 'Bracklesham beds' above the Bagshot beds. The Bracklesham group contains a formation (the Windlesham formation) that is not logged in any of the borehole records I examined, but since it is found not far away in Surrey it might also be present in Berkshire (perhaps as 'Bracklesham beds'). Thirteen boreholes logged quite thick beds of sand above chalk, Reading beds or London clay: some of these may have found Bagshot or Camberley sand. Moreover, as the Camberley Sand formation used to be known as the 'Upper Bagshot beds', it is possible that some 'Bagshot' records would now be assigned to the Camberley sand. All of this is a matter for far better geologists than me.

Few boreholes north of a line drawn along the Kennet record 'Bagshot beds' until we pass east of Reading, where they are more common (though not widespread) north of that line. South of that line they are found across Berkshire. The formation describes layers of fine to coarse-grained sand in a range of colours, with clay bands in some areas and mica bands in others, that can contain glauconite and narrow seams of gravel. There may be a thick bed of multicoloured clay at the top (the Swinley Clay member). All of this suggests that the formation was laid down not far offshore. The Coombes at Barkham *(see Appendix 4 for directions)* has an attractive circular walk around which you can see the Bagshot formation at outcrop *(see Photo 4.7)* and some of the sixth terrace of the Blackwater *(see Chapter 5).*

Photo 4.7: The Coombes, Barkham: Bagshot formation

The Camberley Sand formation was first given its own place in the BGS hierarchy in 1999. Sandy layers of the 'Barton beds' and the 'upper Bagshot sands' are now regarded as constituting this formation. The first clear identification of it is at a BGS borehole near Bracknell (in the log for which it is recorded as 'Bracklesham beds'; but this is one of the two BGS reference sections for this formation). Typically, it begins at a thick bed of mainly flinty gravel (the Stanners Hill pebble bed) and contains homogeneous yellow-brown sand, which has occasionally conglomerated to form a white sandstone; sometimes ironstones are found. At the Devil's Highway near Crowthorne (a Roman road – *see Chapter 6 and Appendix 4 for directions*), the Camberley sand outcrops and iron staining is visible in the face and the many red flints washed out from it, but when fresh (as can be seen in the path) it is a very fine, pale yellow, unconsolidated sand.

Photo 4.8: The Devil's Highway, Crowthorne

Photo 4.9: Fresh Camberley sand

Barton Group

While it is uncertain whether this is present under Berkshire, if it were it would be greeny-grey clay containing shells, sand and some glauconite, it would weather to yellow and it might have flint beds in lower layers. If present, the sand would be fine.

5

The Quaternary Period

THIS PERIOD COVERS, broadly, the last 2.6 million years. Although tectonic plates have continued to move, the world has not changed nearly so much in the Quaternary as in the earlier, much longer periods described in previous chapters. For a British reader, the most significant developments would be the existence of a land bridge to Europe and the bursting of a huge post-glacial lake in the North Sea, drowning Doggerland and the land bridge and opening the English Channel. In Berkshire, the landscape changed during the Pleistocene: western and north-western Britain rose, causing the western London Basin to rise to around 180metres higher than the Suffolk coast. Throughout the Tertiary period south-eastern England had been flat, but major, rapid climate change saw low-temperature erosion followed by floods carry eroded material across the surface, scouring valleys. Much of Berkshire is covered with these 'superficial deposits' (earth, sand, clay and other materials that have not been laid down long enough, or buried deeply enough, to turn to stone). The older, deeper, harder materials described in earlier chapters are often called 'bedrock'.

During this period cycles of warm and cool climate repeated – seventeen are recognised, ten of them during the last million years. The cycles each lasted for about 100,000 years, and for three of the four most recent cycles there is evidence of ice sheets having covered northern Britain. During the Anglian sub-age *(see Appendix 2)* the Thames was diverted southwards from the Vale of St Albans to its current position, although the glaciers themselves reached no closer to Berkshire than Moreton-in-Marsh to the west and Aylesbury to the east. The most recent glaciation peaked between 23,000 and 14,000 years ago and the ice had largely melted by 13,000 years ago (although another glaciation, brief in geological terms – about 1,000 years – covered Wales, the Lake District and Scotland from about 11,000 years ago). In Berkshire, no glacial deposits are present but fluvial deposits follow the Thames, the Kennet, the Blackwater–Loddon and the Colne.

Meanwhile, during the Wolstonian sub-age *(see Appendix 2 and Chapter 6)* Neanderthals had arrived in Britain, though they were not the first hominids to do so, and they left and returned several times over the next 350,000 years. *Homo sapiens* arrived between 40,000 and 50,000 years ago.

Ice Ages and rivers

Though no glaciers came to Berkshire, during the Pleistocene many of the river terraces around the Thames and other rivers were laid down; other major rivers were laid down and/or changed their courses, drawn by the Thames; and both winds and outwash from melting glaciers formed much of the landscape.

As a river flows towards the sea it picks up and lays down silts, sands and gravels in different areas. In steep terrain it flows swiftly, meanders relatively little and wears away or breaks off rock and soil that it passes over; as slopes reduce it slows down, meanders more and drops the heavier and/or bulkier material it is carrying; in more nearly level areas it flows more gently, meanders even more and drops the light material, and thus a floodplain builds up to one or both sides. From time to time, storms send a surge of water flowing rapidly down the river, increasing erosion everywhere it reaches. River terraces record where material was dropped during long periods of gentle flow and later cut through during long periods of stronger flow.

Such periods can occur during ice ages. In cold (glacial) periods, water is bound up in ice, so the sea level drops, which increases river gradients and thus flow; so where a river is still flowing it cuts a deeper channel. Chunks of ice breaking off and flowing down the channel might have had a similar effect. When water flows over chalk, it dissolves the chalk and frees up any flint, which might be carried along, eroded in its turn or broken up in storm surges, gradually becoming gravel that takes on a rounded profile; when water flows over sand beds it carries off grains of sand and breaks up, wears away then carries off any stones bedded in the sand (such as sarsens). When the climate starts to warm (interglacial periods) the ice melts, and at first flow rates vastly increase. New channels start to be cut and existing ones widen and deepen. Most people remark that British river valleys are often much wider than the rivers currently running through them; partly this is because rivers change their course so may run on one side of a valley for a time then cut new channels on the other side; partly it is because rivers were probably much bigger in the early parts of interglacial periods. Over time sea levels rose, river gradients grew shallower, flow rates reduced and floodplains started to build up again, out of the sands and pebbles freed during the previous glacial period. Come another glacial period, a new channel started to be cut through the new floodplain, carrying material downstream and leaving a river terrace behind that could be much higher than the level of the new channel, especially where continued tectonic uplift (such as the collision driving up the Alps and the slow rebound of land that has been crushed under glaciers or permafrost) is changing the gradient.

Figure 5.1 shows the terraces at two points along the north bank of the Thames. The figure shows the channel of the Thames cutting deeper, and changing its course, to where it now runs. The terrace at Nettlebed (some 170metres above the present bed of the Thames) is believed to be the oldest of these terraces. Some terraces are believed to have been laid down at about the same time, e.g. while the Freeland terraces were being laid down west of Oxford, at Slough (several miles east and nearly 50metres lower) the Black Park terraces were being laid down; the Boyn Hill terraces (Maidenhead) are younger than the Black Park, and believed to be contemporary with the Orsett Heath terraces east of London. At Northmoor, about six miles west of Oxford, the river has cut a deep channel, largely filled with gravels (the grey areas) and silt-and-sand 'alluvium' (the yellow areas). By the time it reaches Shepperton the channel is some 50metres lower, and the alluvium has thickly covered the gravels. This may show floodplains being laid down in periods of gentler flow.

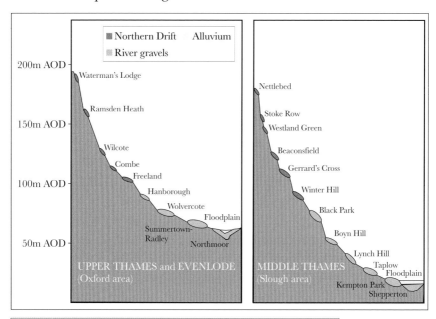

Figure 5.1: Terraces at two points along the River Thames
Redrawn by author from Sumbler, 1996

Figure 5.1 also shows that the channel has gradually moved southwards: it now flows around nine miles south of Beaconsfield, for example. During the early Pleistocene the Thames flowed north-eastwards from around Reading through what is now East Anglia; and the Evenlode (which joins it near Oxford) drained a much larger area than it does now, and brought south pebbles (some quite large) from the Midlands and possibly even north Wales ('Northern Drift' in Figure 5.1). As a result of the Anglian glaciation the Thames changed its course, eventually flowing a little north of eastwards from near Maidenhead to about Clacton-on-Sea, where it joined the Medway to flow quite sharply north-east. The present mouth of the Thames dates back around 8,000 years, after the English Channel was created when a vast, post-glacial lake in what is now the North Sea burst its banks.

The pebbles in the Northern Drift found west of Oxford come from the Triassic Kidderminster Formation (sandstones, quartz and quartzites), among other types of rock. The Kesgrave sands and gravels found in Essex contain similar amounts of a similar quartzite. This is our evidence for the pre-Anglian course of the Thames. The Northern Drift also contains small quantities of igneous pebbles, and one theory suggests that the igneous content entered the Evenlode as a result of several glaciations in north Wales.

A good view of three, perhaps four, terraces can be gained from Winter Hill, just across the river from Marlow:

Photo 5.1: View of the River Thames from Winter Hill

If you look at the ridge in the background, over which the A404 is disappearing, this gives an idea of the size of the Thames valley at Marlow. The viewpoint *(see Appendix 4 for directions)* is on the top of the Winter Hill gravel terrace on the southern bank, which was laid down late in the Anglian stage. In Photo 5.2 I have highlighted the Shepperton gravel terrace (1 – late Devensian), the Taplow gravel terrace (2 – late Wolstonian) and the Winter Hill terrace on the northern bank (3). Photo 5.3 shows the Taplow and

Winter Hill terraces further downstream, and what may be either a bit of an older terrace behind, or an extension of the Winter Hill terrace that, perhaps, a stream has cut through:

Photos 5.2 and 5.3: Views of the River Thames from Winter Hill

The following table looks at those of the river terraces shown in Figure 5.1 that appear around the northern border of Berkshire, and shows when we believe they were laid down:

Age (Ka):	Epoch:	Stages:		Age of deposit (Ka):	Deposit:	
		Glacial:	Warmer:		Type/ name:	RGT:
Now	HOLO-CENE		Fland-rian		Soils, river deposits, human detritus	
~34	PLEISTOCENE	Deven-sian		~115	Shepperton	1
					Kempton Park	2
~110			Ipswich-ian			
~130		Wol-stonian		~230	Taplow	3
					Lynch Hill	4
					Boyn Hill	5
~352			Hoxnian			
~424		Anglian		~476	Black Park	6
					Winter Hill	7
~800				~750	Gerrard's Cross	8
			Cromer-ian		Beacons-field	9
					Westland Green	10
NOTE:	Extracted and organised by me from Berkshire Geoconservation (2009) and website.					

In the table, 'Ka' stands for thousands of years before the present; 'RGT' stands for River Gravel Terrace number (a system in use to relate the age of terraces that are found in different places or have more than one name). The two age columns come from different sources and do not match during the Devensian. The RGT numbers suggest that the Kempton Park gravels are earlier than the Shepperton gravels (though this should be treated with caution).[*] I've looked at the Thames in detail; Berkshire Geoconservation has

---

[*] The BGS Quaternary system *(see below)* renumbers the Taplow, Kempton Park and Shepperton terraces 2, 1 and unnumbered, so that it can insert a Hackney terrace and give it RGT 3.

constructed tables on a similar system for two other rivers in the county:

Age (Ka):	Epoch:	Stages:		RGT:	River:	
		Glacial:	Warmer:		Kennet:	Loddon/ B'water:
Now	HOLO-CENE		Fland-rian		Soils, river deposits, human detritus	
~34	PLEISTOCENE	Deven-sian		1	Heale's Lock	See below, unnamed
				2	Been-ham Grange	Unnamed
~110			Ipswich-ian			
~130		Wol-stonian		3	That-cham	Unnamed
				4	–	Unnamed
				5	Ham-stead Marshall	Remnant
~352			Hoxnian			
~424		Anglian		6	Silches-ter	Remnant
				7	Been-ham stocks	Unnamed
~800		Cromer-ian		8	Buck-lebury Com-mon	Black-water only
				9	Cold Ash	–
				10	–	–
NOTE:	Extracted and organised by me from McMillan et al. (2011) and BG website.					

The table shows that during some periods in which two or even three different channels were cut by the Thames (leaving terraces behind) only one or two were cut by the Kennet (or the Loddon, or the Blackwater). The names used in the Kennet column are those of particular types of aggregates (all should be followed by 'gravel' and are assigned **member** status by the BGS). Other researchers have found what would probably be RGT 4 on this system (near Taplow). The Loddon/Blackwater terraces have not been named, and some are greatly depleted ('remnants'). Neither for the Kennet, nor for the Loddon/Blackwater, is terrace 1 clearly distinguishable from the present floodplain. The names give an indication of how the course of the Kennet has changed over time, and the table below expands on this:

RGT:	Kennet:	Heights:	Loddon/ Blackwater:	Heights:
9	Cold Ash		–	–
8	Bucklebury Common	140–122 metres	Blackwater only	104–998 metres
7	Beenham stocks	108–100 metres	Unnamed	
6	Silchester	114–78 metres	Remnant	85–78 metres
5	Hamstead Marshall		Remnant	68–55 metres
4	–	–	Unnamed	65–48 metres
3	Thatcham	80–42 metres	Unnamed	62–35 metres
2	Beenham Grange	75–28 metres	Unnamed	52–25 metres
1	Heale's Lock	NA	Unnamed	NA
NOTE:	Extracted and organised by me from BG website; three terraces recognised by the BGS do not appear on that site.			

In the table the 'heights' columns show the highest and lowest points along the river that this terrace has been found: the Silchester gravels have occasionally been found higher above OSD than the (older) Beenham stocks, for example. Conversely, terraces 2 and 3 are occasionally found below current ground level. Comparable ranges could be given for terrace 1, but would only indicate how the height of the floodplain varies. Researchers disagree about the Hamstead Marshall terrace, so I have not suggested a height for it.

Chartres (1981) carried out a detailed study of the Kennet river terraces and found that the Beenham Grange and Heale's Lock terraces were laid down in beds (like river deposits in 'normal' times) while the Thatcham, Silchester and Beenham terraces showed clear boundaries between **periglacial** layers (gravels held in a clay matrix) and later layers (silty, then sandy matrices). These later silts and sands (and those in the younger terraces) contained unusual minerals not present either in the clay-supported layers or in Palæogene layers below them, which might have been blown in (by wind) from the North Sea basin, after the Devensian period.

Newell *et al.* (2015) studied the Lambourn, finding that Devensian scouring of the river valley created a thick layer of shattered chalk, some of which later dissolved to a thick clay surrounding the remaining chalk gravel. The valley filled with thick layers of gravel during the Loch Lomond stadial (the last cold period during the Devensian stage: ice ages (stages) may be glacial or interglacial, and stages are in turn divided into cold stadials and warmer interstadials). The Loch Lomond stadial started about 12,500 years ago and lasted about 200 years (different dates are sometimes given to this period, which is also known as the Younger Dryas after an alpine plant, *dryas octopetala*). This process may also have occurred in larger river valleys (such as the Kennet's); but few or no chalk pebbles have been found in Kennet terraces, perhaps because much more water would have flowed through its valley, carrying the gravels further and dissolving the chalk more rapidly. The point is that the shattered-chalk-and-clay base layer is relatively impermeable: much of the Lambourn valley is still wetland and water meadows around both the Kennet and the Lambourn were significant for the Tudor economy of Berkshire *(see Chapter 6)*.

To pull all of this together, we must remember that before the Anglian stage the ground may have been much less hilly than it is now. Figure 5.2 shows how the rivers changed course over time:

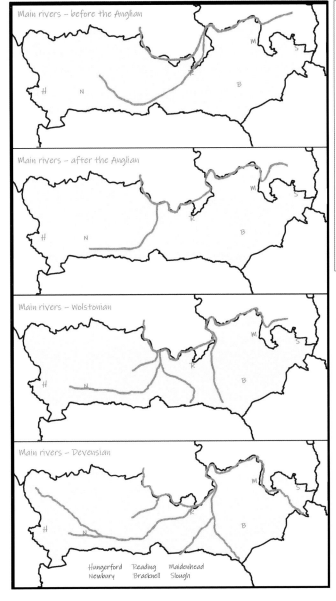

Figure 5.2: How the courses of the main rivers changed during the Quaternary

Redrawn by author from Wymer (1999), Hosfield (2007), McMillan *et al.* (2011) and Newell *et al.* (2015)

Before the Anglian glaciation, the Thames and the Kennet were much smaller rivers flowing from north to south, then eastwards to the sea in East Anglia, possibly around present-day Ipswich. Many of the headwaters of the proto-Thames had been captured by the new River Soar during the Neogene, beginning the process of driving the river southwards. During the Anglian, its drainage via St Albans was blocked by glaciers, accelerating this process, which was completed during the Devensian glaciation. At some point (perhaps after the Anglian: compare the second and third panels *in Figure 5.2*) it cut the Goring gap *(see Photo 5.4)*, separating the Downs from the Chilterns. As the Thames moved southwards, the mouth of the Kennet moved first westwards (along what is now the Sulham valley), then eastwards again as the Pang began to drain the high ground south and west of the Goring Gap, and the Kennet's headwaters began to shift southwards and westwards. The proto-Loddon is believed to have joined the Kennet north of Aldermaston during the Wolstonian. The proto-Blackwater flowed north to Shiplake, remaining insignificant until the Wolstonian and capturing the Loddon from the Kennet during the Devensian. During and after this final glacial period the Lambourn began to drain the high valleys in the west that had started to be carved after the Anglian, joining the Kennet near Thatcham.

Photo 5.4: The Goring gap, looking from Lough Down

Other effects of Ice Ages

Although, *as mentioned in Chapter 1,* glaciers did not extend as far as Berkshire, various periglacial effects can be seen.

During cold, dry periods of the Pleistocene loess began to accumulate south of glaciated areas. This is wind-built drifts of fine-grained material, and the 'brickearths' found in some river terraces may be loess.[†] It may also have contributed to the slope deposits found in the Berkshire Downs. Frost-weathered detritus is believed to have formed a slurry with glacial meltwater and flowed downhill, notably into the coombes in the Downs. These slope deposits built up over long periods, sometimes over more than one glaciation, and layers laid down in warmer, interglacial periods may appear between the glacial layers.

Other slope deposits built up from sand, clay and stones washed off or out from under melting glaciers; the term 'head' is often used for material eroded during colder periods and washed out during warmer ones. Coombe deposits can be head that is mostly eroded chalk. Another kind, widespread in the Berkshire Downs, is clay-with-flints and I will say more about this later in this chapter. Head was laid down in layers and the surfaces between them are sometimes distinct.

Permafrost south of the glaciers has left a number of marks on the landscape. 'Dry' valleys appear to have no water in them now but actually were carved by streams that could not penetrate the frozen ground. You can drive (or cycle) along a good example at Radley Bottom: *see Appendix 4 for directions*. Various holes in chalk and other rock have later been filled by relatively loose sediments (such as Lambeth Group sands). Some were formed by freezing:

◊ 'pingos', large frozen domes which formed beneath the ground surface then grew as artesian wells added water from underneath (it is believed) – these later melted, leaving holes *(see Photo 8.3 for possible examples)*,

◊ wedges opened by freezing water, which later could provide a starting point for solution cavities *(see below)*,

◊ cracks caused by cold-related shrinking, which can form wide networks in clays and silts and

◊ bulges and other distortions in gravel beds,

[†] Chartres (1981) did not think the wind-borne material he found in the Kennet river terraces was loess.

while others were formed during or as a result of thawing:

◊   solution cavities *(see Photos 5.5 and 5.6)*, where meltwater has dissolved chalk – two notable kinds are 'pipes' (as the name suggests, long tubular holes that are often vertical or nearly vertical) and 'swallow holes' that can be several metres deep – there is a good example of the latter near Hurley *(see Appendix 4 for directions)*,

◊   where the surface thawed meltwater lakes built up behind still-frozen dams (for example, rocks warm up more slowly than loose sediments or soil) and when these burst large volumes of water flowed out, meaning great force and scouring action, cutting deep, often v-shaped, channels and

Photos 5.5 and 5.6: Owl Pit, near Stanford Dingley: two solution cavities filled with Upnor Formation sands

◊ the ground thawed more slowly (permafrost can extend dozens of metres into the ground) and shrinkage cracks opened (because water occupies less space than ice), into which meltwater flowed, carrying minerals that might be different from the minerals in the host rock or sediment.

Changes in hydrostatic pressure (for example where the weight of ice or the expansion of a section freezing put pressure on unfrozen water) may have injected sands, clays, even pebbles into gaps such as those referred to above, or between layers of coarser and finer material.

There are other effects on relatively unconsolidated sediments such as sands, clays and gravels. Ground surfaces subject to permafrost are often notably hummocky. Another is frost-sorting, which affects beds of unsorted stones. Where stones have been in rivers for a long time, they are gradually smoothed, graded by size and tend to all point in a similar direction. Frost-sorted beds are made up of angular **clasts** of many different sizes, pointing in many different directions and sometimes bedded in a matrix of sands or clays. Over repeated freeze–thaw cycles, water expanding when it freezes moves the clasts to create room and gradually they end up all pointing in the same direction (usually upwards). Often this does not sort them in any other way (i.e. they remain a collection of many different sizes and shapes).

Quaternary deposits in Berkshire

Quaternary beds were found in 72% of the 492 boreholes for which I collated BGS data *(see Chapter 1)*, and the following summary might interest some readers:

Layers:	Superficial deposits:			All Quaternary:
Mainly:	Gravel beds	Clays	Other	
Found in:	38%	17%	42%	72%
Thickest bed:	11.6 metres	7.1 metres	9 metres	11.6 metres
Narrowest bed:	0.9 metres	1 metre	0.15 metre	0.15 metre
Median thickness:	3.7 metres	2.3 metres	1 metre	3.7 metres

'Superficial' is used to describe sands, clays, silts, gravels and peat of Quaternary date that are still unconsolidated, that is, have begun the process of turning into stone but not proceeded far. 'Other' lumps together soil, ground 'made' by builders or farmers and various kinds of periglacial deposit *(see above)*. Chapter 4 mentions potential problems with the identification of some of these clay and gravel beds, for example that 'Barton beds' are now allotted to the Bracklesham Group if they are sands and the Quaternary if they are mainly clay. So, to look at Figure 5.3 for

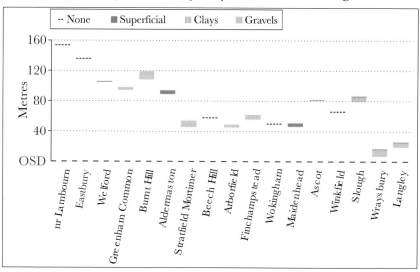

Figure 5.3: Quaternary layers found in seventeen boreholes
Drawn by author from British Geological Survey data

example, the relatively thick clay deposit found at Finchampstead might belong to the (Eocene) Barton Group.

Figure 5.3 completes the diagram that was begun with Figure 2.4 and continued in Figures 3.1 and 4.2. As we saw in the last of these, in six of these boreholes either no Quaternary layers remain or those that do were not worth recording (in the opinion of the people digging the borehole). Apart from giving some impression of Berkshire's contours and the fall of the Thames from Maidenhead to Wraysbury, this figure shows how on hilltops and ridges quite deep gravels can be found but soil and other superficial layers tend to be shallower than in valleys,[‡] and how periglacial or river-borne gravel is found over much of the county.

In 2011 the BGS published a formal **lithostratigraphic** scheme for Quaternary deposits in Great Britain and the Isle of Man, and the parts that apply to Berkshire are as follows.

Age (Ka):	*Traditional nomenclature:*	*Current nomenclature:*		
–	Superficial, made ground	Britannia catchments group	Thames catchments subgroup	Maidenhead formation
~12	Head, drift, plateau gravel, valley gravel			Kennet valley formation
~600	Clay, silt, sand, gravel	Residual deposits group	Kesgrave catchment subgroup	Sudbury formation
				Clay-with-flints formation
~3,400	NEOGENE PERIOD			
NOTE:	Extracted and organised by me from McMillan *et al.* (2011).			

The Blackwater–Loddon terraces and layers around the rivers Colne, Mole and Wey are assigned to the Maidenhead formation. Some of the older Thames terraces between Goring and Slough are

---

[‡]   Burnt Hill is in a high valley.

assigned to the Sudbury formation.[§]

'*Clay with flints*'

I am interested in this because my garden is on 'clay with flints'. Of the 492 borehole logs I examined:

Thickness of 'clay with flints':	On hills:	On rivers:	Total:	
< 2metres	13	3	16	3%
2–5metres	9	2	11	2%
> 5metres	3	1	4	1%
Total:	25 (5%)	6 (1%)	31	6%

Although boreholes find 'clay with flints' across Berkshire, most included in my table were in the hilly north-west. Confusingly, there are two definitions of the term: a narrow one (reddish smectitic clay containing nodular flints) and a broad one (a wide range of clays, containing flints and other river deposits). The narrow definition covers both Neogene and Quaternary layers. This table reflects the broad definition and so some of the many boreholes recording 'ballast', 'drift' and a few other terms should probably be added to it.

Gravels

In Chapters 2 and 4 I wrote about clays, silts and sands. Gravels are rounded or angular (often broken) fragments of rock, where most of the fragments present are between 2 and 64mm in diameter; where between 64 and 256mm they are called cobbles and where greater than 256mm boulders. Note that, as with clays and silts, we are talking about 'most of the fragments present': a gravel bed may contain pebbles, cobbles and boulders. Where all the fragments are similar in size, it is called 'well sorted'; moderately well sorted and

---

[§]   Possibly also the Cold Ash and Bucklebury Common terraces of the Kennet, though this is unclear.

poorly sorted are two other categories often used. Fragments that have travelled a long way, or for a long time, tend to become rounder and smoother (though often chatter marks can still be seen in their surfaces, telling stories of other fragments they banged into during this process); where a fragment has one or more recently broken face and/or sharpish edges, it is called 'angular'. However, rather than using different names for different kinds of fragment, geologists often lump all fragments together under the catch-all name 'clasts'.

Gravels tend to reflect local geology, so for instance west of Reading (the Kennet valley and the high ground either side of it) the gravels are mostly flint and pieces of quartz and sarsen; Thames terraces also contain Jurassic limestone from Oxfordshire; the Blackwater and the Loddon carry in sandstones from the Lower Greensand in Hampshire and Surrey. But periglacial gravels can have come a long way: Northern Drift clasts can come from Gloucestershire (limestone), north Wales (quartzite) or well into the Midlands (Sherwood sandstone). The Thames gravels contain well-travelled material; the Kennet gravels are almost all local and the Loddon/Blackwater gravels mostly local.

Gravel is mined in open pits, which are usually shallow (compared to quarries, say) and nowadays a licence to extract gravel is usually granted only on condition that the site be 'restored' once economic extraction has been completed. This means either filling in the pit and adding a layer of soil (so it can be grassed over or used for farming) or leaving it to fill up naturally and become a lake (for fishing or boating, usually). Although they are not very likely to reveal much original geology now, many worked-out gravel pits in Berkshire have been converted to visitor sites and four well worth visiting are the Thatcham Nature Discovery Centre (for reedbeds, alder woodland, fen), Dinton Pastures Country Park at Hurst, near Wokingham (for lakes, woods, aquatic wildlife), Moor Green Lakes at Eversley Cross, near Crowthorne (for lakes and birdwatching) and the SSSI at Wraysbury and Hythe End Gravel Pits (lakes, woods, birdwatching – and some unworked areas of floodplain gravel).

6

Berkshire archæology

N THE INTRODUCTION, I said that geology can seem like long, complicated lists of 'what happened when' and suggested that we need to keep our eye on all three parts of this description at once. The same is true of archæology and history. If an archæologist finds something there are now quite a lot of ways to suggest to us 'what' it might be and to put a date on it *(discussed in the next paragraph)*, but what caused it to exist, and to be where it was found? Moreover, a date (or range of dates) is only one aspect of 'when': what else was going on at the same time? The Quaternary period was a time of major climate change, which affected the appearance of the land and rivers, where the sea was and what animals and plants could survive and where. We need to understand what conditions early humans faced if we are to understand why they moved and settled where they did, when they did and what consequences their moving and settling had, both for the landscape and for human development within that landscape.

Before I start, we should consider how an archæologist works out how old human finds might be. Most of us have heard of [14]carbon dating, but this is increasingly unreliable where the find is more than 40,000 years old. We can work out when flint was knapped (or an animal butchered) by luminescence dating if the find has been burned, but if it has not we need to look at context. Has the site been buried by a layer that can be dated (of volcanic ash, say)? We know when some animals appeared in or disappeared from particular areas, so identifying a bone can be helpful. Can we find pollen, plant remains or the remains of insects or molluscs (snails, say) at the site, to give us a clue? Are wooden remains present, large enough and in good enough condition for tree-ring dating? We know roughly when river gravels were laid down, so finds in gravels can give us a rough idea when an artefact was made or an animal butchered – but possibly not where (since a river may have carried the artefact or bone to where we found it). Rivers may also erode older terraces and redeposit them downstream, so objects or bones may be found in layers younger than they are. We know roughly when some flint-knapping styles began, or new designs for, say, hand-axes were adopted, but these are only rough guides because it took time for new approaches to spread. Moreover, like today, not everybody adopted new technology when it became available and many people valued old and tried objects and technology (my grandmother's spear, my grandfather's quernstone) and continued to use them long after others had moved on to new approaches.

Human prehistory

At long intervals during the Pleistocene epoch, Palæolithic hunters would venture into Berkshire, leaving tools and very occasionally butchered remains behind them. The first visits were (we believe) between 430,000 and 450,000 years before the present (BP), early in the Anglian sub-age. As we have seen, during the Anglian glaciers covered more of Britain than at any time since; most trees, herbs and shrubs would have been killed by cold and drought (ice ages are extremely dry) and, though not under ice, Berkshire would have resembled arctic tundra. Animals adapted to the cold – mammoths, deer, bison – and some survivors of warmer times – straight-tusked elephants, hippopotami, rhinoceros – existed along with a range of predators – hyenas, lions, bears. Britain was still joined to continental Europe, and cold, hungry hunter-gatherers (possibly *Homo heidelbergensis*) would have walked across and back in search of food and shelter. Anglian artefacts have been found, but the date and placing problems I mentioned apply in spades to Figure 6.1.

To take the Kennet as an example, we know roughly when it changed course, and we can put rough dates on the flint tools and shards found near its courses; but compare the first two panels in Figure 6.1. Three of the early Anglian findspots are close to the proto-Kennet (if more than a mile from it is 'close', as the hunter walks); but what about the three findspots at Hamstead Marshall and Wash Common? Now, during the Hoxnian, the proto-Kennet ran further south than it does today, so all six groups of tools might have been carried by the river to where we found them some (considerable) time after their Palæolithic creators left them, and possibly carried some distance, too. This should be remembered for all the findspots in Figure 6.1.

I have not included contour lines in Figure 6.1 because before the Anglian stage the ground may have been much less hilly than it is now. To put this another way, the contours we now see were carved into a plain, over a long time that might have started before the period covered by Figure 6.1 and continued after it, by rivers and periglacial run-off.

Later Anglian finds at Caversham are close to two spots along the proto-Thames (Caversham and Emmer Green). Caversham is interesting, because there have been many Palæolithic finds (some extensive) in and around what is now Caversham. However, they may have been brought there by the Thames and we are talking of a time-span of perhaps 100,000 years (well into the Hoxnian stage – *see Appendix 3*), so it is a bit of a stretch to talk of this site being 'favoured' by Palæolithic visitors. For these reasons I've included them in the second panel, with other finds dated to the Hoxnian stage.

Glacial stages were long – averaging 100,000 years or so – but warmer, interglacial stages were relatively short – typically 10,000 to 15,000 years. Geological sub-ages often contained both glacial and interglacial stages; sometimes more than one of each. As glaciers melted sea levels would rise and, as we have seen, rivers would grow in both size and power to deal with melting ice and occasional floods as temporary melt-water lakes burst their banks. More temperate vegetation would spread back in (rapidly, in geological terms) and animals would, too, as they found their way across the

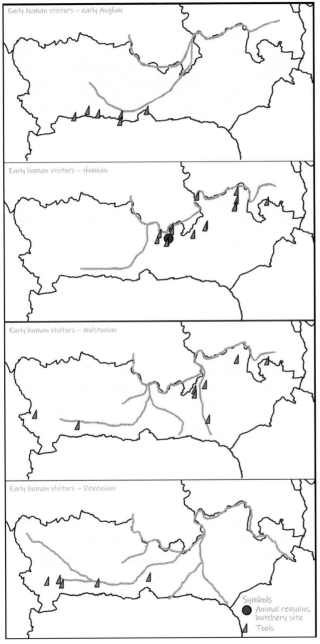

Figure 6.1:
Early human
visits: Palæo-
lithic findspots

River map
redrawn
by author
from Wymer
(1999), Hos-
field (2007),
McMillan *et
al.* (2011) and
Newell *et al.*
(2015)

land bridge that still joined what is now the British Isles to Europe. Where the animals went, hunters might follow. Later Palæolithic artefacts have been found along the Thames, dating to the Hoxnian (interglacial) and possibly the early years of the Wolstonian sub-age that followed it *(third panel in Figure 6.1)*, some close to and others perhaps away from the river. The Wolstonian was a long sub-age – more than 300,000 years – and more than one glaciation occurred during it. The Thames eventually joined the Rhine and the Seine to form a vast Channel river that closed the more southerly routes from the Continent: the route to the British Isles now ran down from what later became Scandinavia and Germany, across Doggerland. For over 100,000 years no evidence of early human presence in Britain has been found.

Late in the Pleistocene epoch, however, possibly while the final, Devensian ice sheets were receding *(see Appendix 2)*, hunters began to make regular visits to a few sites in the Kennet valley. These would have been *Homo sapiens*. An Upper Palæolithic site at Avington (near Kintbury) has been dated (by optically stimulated luminescence, OSL) to 10,250 BP, ±1,100, and sites around Thatcham may be of comparable age. These are all riverside sites: the fourth panel in Figure 6.1 shows the length of the Kennet that we can be certain about (based on river terrace deposits) but its headwaters probably extended much further – *compare with Figure 6.2*.

Judging by evidence of the making of large numbers of flint tools, 'a significant concentration' (Chisham, 2006) of sites spread along the Kennet between Thatcham and Hungerford during the Early Mesolithic. Other, probably riverine, Mesolithic sites have been found east of the Kennet valley, at Binfield (on the Blackwater), Wokingham (on the Loddon) and Bray, Earley, Reading and Windsor (on the Thames), among other places. Two of the western sites (Thatcham, Wawcott [also near Kintbury]) continued to be used at intervals into the Neolithic, and display evidence of occupation (post holes at Thatcham, a hearth at Wawcott). Also, the Lambourn was clearly followed up into the Berkshire Downs. There is more evidence of settlement during the Neolithic, buildings have been found (causewayed enclosures at Eton, Runnymede and Horton, near Slough, and four 'houses' at the latter) and the first examples of boundary making (ring ditches at Reading and Horton). Several kinds of barrow appear, some in extensive groups (at Lambourn, Inkpen, Wash Common and

Ufton Nervet) and cursus monuments at Sonning and possibly also Avington (these were long parallel earthworks, possibly used for competitions).

Barrows continued to be built during the early and middle

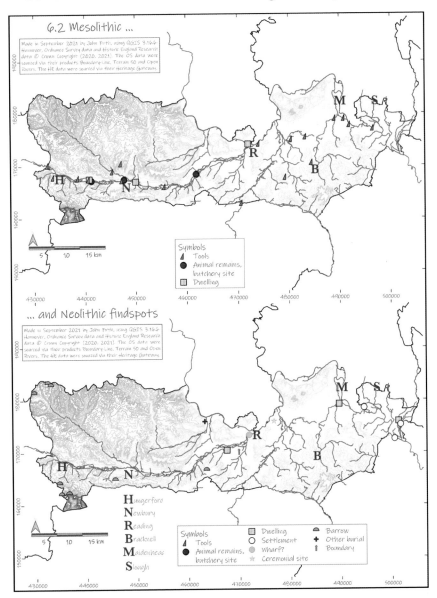

periods of the Bronze Age (between about 4,500 BP and about 3,200 BP), but compared to nearby counties relatively few other sites have been discovered in Berkshire. Several settlement sites from the Late Bronze Age have been found, however. Hoards are

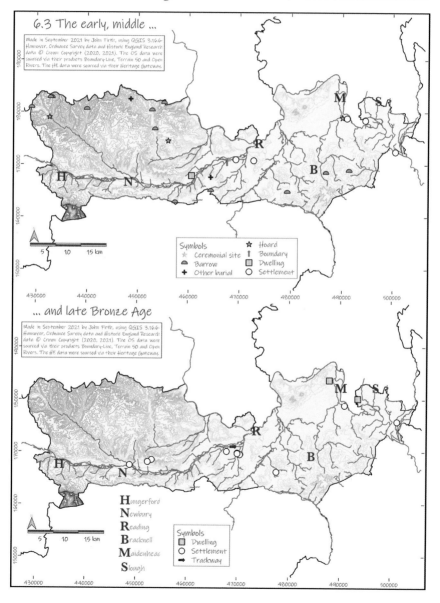

6.3 The early, middle ...

Made in September 2021 by John Firth, using QGIS 3.16.6-
Hannover. Ordnance Survey data and Historic England Research
data © Crown Copyright (2020, 2021). The OS data were
sourced via their products Boundary-Line, Terrain 50 and Open
Rivers. The HE data were sourced via their Heritage Gateway.

Symbols
☆ Hoard
⭐ Ceremonial site
⬟ Barrow
✚ Other burial
⚑ Boundary
⬜ Dwelling
○ Settlement

... and late Bronze Age

Made in September 2021 by John Firth, using QGIS 3.16.6-
Hannover. Ordnance Survey data and Historic England Research
data © Crown Copyright (2020, 2021). The OS data were
sourced via their products Boundary-Line, Terrain 50 and Open
Rivers. The HE data were sourced via their Heritage Gateway.

Hungerford
Newbury
Reading
Bracknell
Maidenhead
Slough

Symbols
⬜ Dwelling
○ Settlement
➡ Trackway

an interesting feature of Bronze Age worship. Often deposited in rivers (as at Bray) or in important sites (the Yattendon Hoard was buried at the top of a hill; the Lambourn Hoard near both the Ridgeway and the source of the Lambourn – *see Photos 3.4 and 3.5*), they often included objects of high value (as at Yattendon and Lambourn), that sometimes had been specially made, and were a type of offering or sacrifice.

Bronze was made from materials found a long way from Berkshire (copper alloyed originally with tin, and later with lead). Bronze workers seem to have been specialists; they may have travelled widely carrying both the materials and the tools of their trade with them. Perhaps because of this bronze did not entirely replace flint and other stones for tool making (though the tools made with stone became much rougher and simpler), and though bronze tools were made and used (notably, for woodworking) the metal was widely used for ornate, valuable, 'prestige' items (such as jewellery, or weapons and armour for show rather than use, both of which are widely found in hoards).

The Bronze Age has been described by English Heritage as one of transition from 'monument-dominated landscapes and mobile settlement patterns to... more permanent settlement and... agricultural production'. Land boundaries (linear ditches and cross-ridge dykes in the Berkshire Downs) appear during the middle and late Bronze Age, as do the first hamlets (Thatcham, Burghfield) and 'trading points' (Runnymede, Burghfield – landing stages on rivers with large numbers of artefacts found near them) – possibly also the first 'hillforts'.

The 'hillforts' that proliferated during the Iron Age appear to have spread east from Wessex and north from Sussex; with one exception at Taplow and one 'possible' near Maidenhead, they do not seem to have crossed the Thames. It is now believed that most of these were not originally fortifications but sites chosen to project a local VIP's prestige and power in a way of life based on farming and family relationships; both arable and animal farming seem to have occurred in and round them. Sometimes they contain stockyards, suggesting a role in allocating animals among the tribe. They are often positioned so as to dominate local paths, tracks (e.g. the Berkshire Ridgeway) and river routes (the Thames, Kennet and Loddon/Blackwater), or at important nodes in field (and perhaps

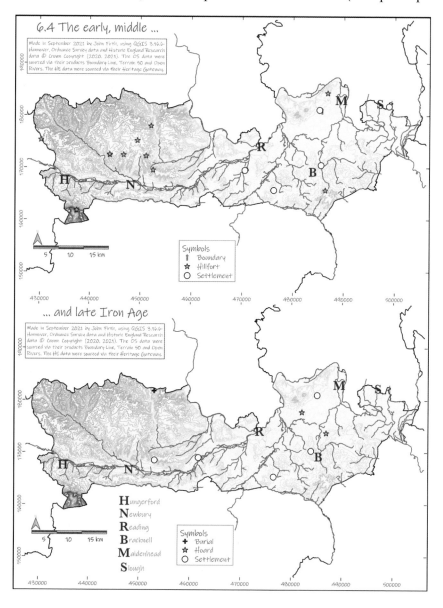

6.4 The early, middle ...

Made in September 2021 by John Firth, using QGIS 3.16.6-Hannover, Ordnance Survey data and Historic England Research data © Crown Copyright (2020, 2021). The OS data were sourced via their products Boundary-Line, Terrain 50 and Open Rivers. The HE data were sourced via their Heritage Gateway.

Symbols
🛡 Boundary
☆ Hillfort
○ Settlement

... and late Iron Age

Made in September 2021 by John Firth, using QGIS 3.16.6-Hannover, Ordnance Survey data and Historic England Research data © Crown Copyright (2020, 2021). The OS data were sourced via their products Boundary-Line, Terrain 50 and Open Rivers. The HE data were sourced via their Heritage Gateway.

Hungerford
Newbury
Reading
Bracknell
Maidenhead
Slough

Symbols
✚ Burial
☆ Hoard
○ Settlement

more territorial) boundaries. The construction and alignment of many suggests display (or sometimes ritual) was more important than defence – few show signs of violence, at least before the Romans arrived – but there is evidence of later strengthening in some (Eton Wick). There were a range of other 'enclosures' *(not shown in Figure 6.4)* – one in a valley, at Padworth, was later strengthened. Because I could think of no way to show them on maps of this scale, I have not included the host of small farmsteads, field boundaries, drove roads and other trackways that covered western and north-eastern Berkshire during the Iron Age.

In the Iron Age little trade (as we understand it) took place as resources were owned by the tribe, not by individuals, but local surpluses were exchanged and sometimes these would have been in part-prepared form (smelted iron: *see below*) or finished goods (pottery). Hillforts seem to have been placed to control networks for distributing such sur-pluses, and also for collecting resources for important communal activities (e.g. feasts, rituals, building, maintaining or improving the hillfort). Storage pits and four-post granaries were sometimes much larger or more numerous than any residents of the 'fort' could have required, and the granaries sometimes were the most visible feature of the 'fort', suggesting a wish to display access to or control of resources and so demonstrate power or prestige.

Iron did not really replace bronze (prestige items continued to be made in bronze throughout the Iron Age) and it took a long time for iron tools and equipment to be widely taken up. Smelting (reducing ore to workable metal) seems to have been carried out *within* many communities, but smithing (making things out of smelted metal) seems to have been a skill confined to specialists, who perhaps travelled *between* communities. Finding the ores was another specialist skill: one early source was iron oxide nodules and coated river gravels (as at Upper Bucklebury: *see Photo 8.1*) and another was the 'iron pan' (conglomerates of river pebbles cemented together with iron oxide) found near Maidenhead and Bracknell *(see Photo 6.1)*.

Photo 6.1: 'Iron pan' nodule, Shurlock Row

The age of invasions

When Claudius invaded Britain in 43CE he claimed (among other things) to be supporting Verica of the Atrebates, who had recently been dispossessed by the Catuvellauni. Calleva Atrebatum (now Silchester), the Roman capital of much of southern Britain, may have been Verica's capital.

Remains of two major roads survive (Ermin Street, running slightly north of westwards, and the road that much later gained the name the Devil's Highway, running slightly north of eastwards). Ermin Street connected Calleva with Corinium – now Cirencester; the Devil's Highway connected it with Londinium. Calleva had a north gate; a road ran from Dorchester to the Roman town at Alchester (which the Romans may have called Alavna); it is believed that the road crossed the Thames and continued to Calleva, and this hypothetical road has been given the name

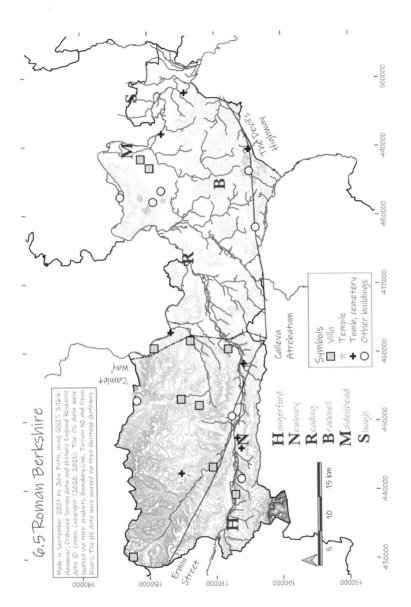

'Camlet Way'; a few short sections of Roman road and some place-
name evidence suggest where it may have run. Minor roads were
laid, but although their general line is sometimes known, only one
Roman milestone has been found (at Finchampstead) and detailed

routes are unclear. Likewise, river trade probably occurred, but Roman ports have yet to be discovered.

Many villas have been found, often on sites long occupied (Lambourn, Kintbury, Thatcham), and some of these may have employed large numbers of people, but to describe them as villages or towns in the modern sense would be misleading. Berkshire seems to have remained mainly farming country, though tiles may have been made around villas, kilns have been found in many possible settlement sites and some weaving tools have been found.

Two temple complexes have been found: at Lowbury Hill near Compton, and at Weycock Hill near Waltham St Lawrence. Comparing Figure 6.5 with earlier maps in this chapter, we see barrows and burials near Lowbury Hill dating back to the early Bronze Age; Waltham St Lawrence had long been settled and an important Iron Age hoard was found nearby.

Calleva may have been abandoned when the Romans left in the fifth century CE, though smaller settlements (Lambourn, Thatcham, Cookham) seem to have continued in use. The first mention of the shire is in 860CE. There is little archæological evidence of Anglo-Saxon Berkshire, though relatively plentiful documentary evidence (charters, mentions in the *Anglo-Saxon Chronicle*, *Domesday Book*). Place-name evidence (the Readas, the Peagas – now Pang) is suggestive rather than conclusive, though the Sunningas are supported by charter evidence. Two churches with Saxon elements survive (Wickham, Stanford Dingley) and several surviving churches are known to have Saxon foundations (Speen, Boxford, Bradfield, Streatley, Sonning, Bray). Berkshire seems to have been argued (and perhaps fought) over by the Mercian and Kentish kingdoms, which may be why Calleva remained small (and possibly abandoned), but the county was West Saxon by Alfred's reign, when a Viking incursion (and fortified camp at Reading) was seen off after battles at Reading, Englefield and Ashdown. (The two latter were fought close to the hypothetical 'Camlet Way', which might support arguments for its existence.) A later incursion, in the tenth century CE, may have seen a battle near Cookham and the fortification of an

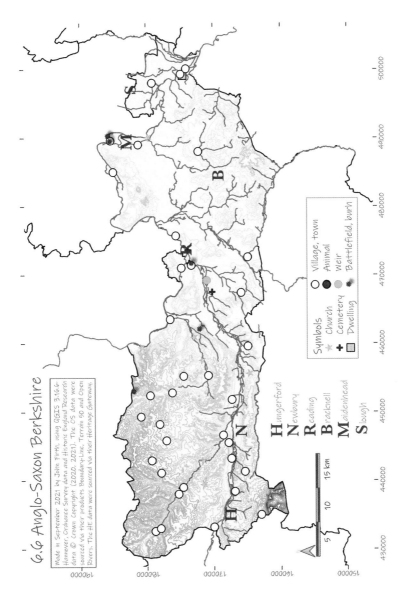

6.6 Anglo-Saxon Berkshire

Made in September 2021 by John Firth, using QGIS 3.16.6-Hannover, Ordnance Survey data and Historic England Research data © Crown Copyright (2020, 2021). The OS data were sourced via their products Boundary-Line, Terrain 50 and Open Rivers. The HE data were sourced via their Heritage Gateway.

Symbols
Village, town ○
Animal ●
Weir ◓
Battlefield, burh ✳
Church ✳
Cemetery ✚
Dwelling ☐

Hungerford
Newbury
Reading
Bracknell
Maidenhead
Slough

island in the Thames (a *burh*) nearby. East and south of Reading seem to have been sparsely settled, the west fairly thickly settled but mainly with dispersed farms and hamlets. Astill (2006; for the Solent Thames Research Framework) writes 'the late Saxon charters paint a picture of a countryside with numerous enclosures, detached areas of woodland in the uplands and meadow lands in the valley', although Lambourn, Newbury, possibly Thatcham, Reading and Cookham grew to something we might describe as a town.

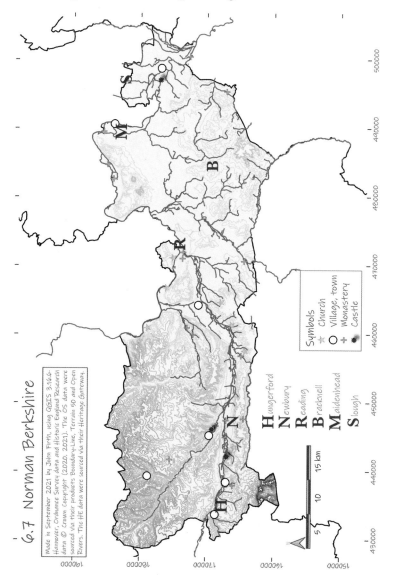

6.7 Norman Berkshire

Made in September 2021 by John Firth, using QGIS 3.16.6-Hannover, Ordnance Survey data and Historic England Research data © Crown Copyright (2020, 2021). The OS data were sourced via their products Boundary-Line, Terrain 50 and Open Rivers. The HE data were sourced via their Heritage Gateway.

Symbols
★ Church
○ Village, town
✦ Monastery
✳ Castle

Hungerford
Newbury
Reading
Bracknell
Maidenhead
Slough

The *Domesday Book* records vast Crown holdings and few Norman barons with much land in Berkshire. Much of the county is described as 'forest'. No major see was based in Berkshire (although the monastery at Abingdon was an important landowner), and for all these reasons medieval documentation is in short supply, compared with the Anglo-Saxon period. There was little assarting (conversion of woodland to pastureland) compared to other counties, except in the (relatively unwooded) valleys of the Thames, Kennet, Loddon and Lambourn. There were monasteries (most of them small preceptories or priories) at Kintbury, Donnington, Sandleford, Poughley, Bradfield, Greenham, Shalford, Reading (three, and the Abbey), Stratfield Saye, Hurley, Bisham (three, at different times), Cookham, Sunningdale (Broomhall) and Wraysbury (Ankerwyke), several of which have connections with the Crusades. A great many churches were built in the twelfth century CE but Astill (2006) tells us 'most of the parish churches are peripheral to villages or are associated with hamlets or farmsteads'. There were really only two castles (Donnington, near Newbury, and Windsor) but around 40 fortified manors or short-lived mottes. The area remained agricultural; some small-scale iron and copper working continued and the 'rise of the sheep' led to textile industries near the larger rivers (for milling). Villages occasionally became towns (we learn this from the issue of borough or market charters in the thirteenth century), sometimes growing naturally and sometimes for other reasons: for example, the Norman foundation of Hungerford at a strategic point along the Kennet Valley, Old Windsor moving to New Windsor when the Castle was built. 'Kennet valley' pottery was produced near Newbury and remains found suggest it was traded widely to the west and north; other potteries operated from Ashampstead and Maidenhead (Camley). Problems in navigating the Thames between Reading and Oxford probably held the former back (for example, Midlands grain was shipped to London from Henley).

The Black Death and after

The arrival of waves of bubonic and other plagues in 1348 saw some villages disappear, but the county seems to have recovered more quickly than many. The redistribution of church lands after the dissolution of the monasteries from 1536 encouraged large-scale agriculture: by the sixteenth century Berkshire was a major supplier of corn to London, at a time when the wool trade was at its height and enclosure of smaller and common lands was beginning. Berkshire began to develop and manage water meadows along its chalk streams and rivers *(see Chapter 3)*. The river or stream was dammed by a weir, led off into carriers along the ridges of a ridge-and-furrow field system, and allowed to flow down the slopes to drains taking it back to the river or stream, further down. Controlled flooding would encourage spring grass (for sheep, or for hay in the autumn followed by aftermath grazing for cattle). Many of the multiple channels we see around the Kennet and Lambourn today are not natural, but relics of that system, which continued well into the eighteenth century.

Trade was both by water and along the twelfth-century Bath Road, which began to see trains of wagons. About 1657 a stagecoach service was introduced. Berkshire was split between the Royalist and Parliamentary sides, and much fought over, during the Civil War and the wool industry declined in the mid- to late seventeenth century, before being reorganised on industrial lines. The opening of turnpike trusts under George I, of mail coaches along the Bath Road, of improvements to navigation along the Kennet (1718–23) and the building of the Kennet and Avon (1794–1810) and Wilts and Berks Canals (1796–1810) all contributed to the trade in wool and corn, as well as enabling coal and timber to be shipped through Berkshire. Hungerford, Newbury and Wokingham all benefited particularly from the Bath Road. The breeding of the black Berkshire pig during the eighteenth century, and the growth of Reading (and its breweries) provided two new streams of trade. The coming of the Great Western Railway (to Maidenhead in 1838;

to Twyford the next year and Reading the year after that) vastly increased the potential for goods carriage, and also made large-scale human travel possible, at a time when roads were still rutted, muddy and often impassable, especially in winter.

If the agricultural revolution benefited those with access to capital, it was at the expense of agricultural labourers. Between around 1760 and 1883 approximately 160,000 acres (around one-third of the county) was enclosed by Parliamentary act, two-thirds of it during and shortly after the Napoleonic Wars (1795–1815). This process abolished commons rights and waste land (to which rights had attached), and transferred enclosed land into private ownership, turning vast numbers of semi-independent peasants into wage labourers with no job security and no right to grow their own food. As to the industrial revolution, the revolutions in industrial organisation had greater effect in Berkshire, at least initially, than the new machinery: large numbers of people exchanged precarious and seasonal employment on the land for precarious all-year-round employment in factories in the growing towns. Likewise, the railway boom benefited some business owners, and allowed people to leave their homes to seek employment, but seriously damaged the road and canal hauliers.

These developments are visible in town buildings – the rows of terraced houses, the factories or mills, the larger number of shops, and the churches and, eventually, schools that were built to serve the incomers. They are also visible in the track/bed, bridges, cuttings and viaducts that carried the canals and then the railways across the county. If the railways and/or canals arrived early, a town benefited (Reading is an example, as is Bracknell) but towns at which they arrived late either suffered or trod water during the eighteenth and nineteenth centuries (Hungerford, Maidenhead, Newbury, Wokingham). Interested readers may wish to study the website of the Berkshire Industrial Archæology group at www.biag.org.uk, which has useful links to a number of other interesting sites.

After the arrival of the motor car in the early twentieth century, and the patenting of tarmacadam in 1902, we can add the roads that now divide and unite the county, and the housing estates (both privately and publicly owned) that spread out from the cities with the transport revolution. Slough (originally a railway town) expanded to its current size after 1925, when the Industrial Estate was founded (for which a large number of very deep boreholes were dug, *as Figure 1.1 shows*). Berkshire is also ringed by airports (for which other deep boreholes were dug), and the proximity of Heathrow has benefited Slough.

As of the 2011 Census, the county's largest towns were Reading (220,000+ inhabitants), Slough (150,000+ inhabitants), Bracknell and Maidenhead (each with more than 60,000 inhabitants) and Wokingham and Newbury (both with more than 35,000 inhabitants). Around 43,000 Berkshire men and women commuted to work in London every day, and more than 24,000 Londoners commuted in the other direction. It will be interesting to see what the 2021 Census shows.

7

Samples

HERE ARE A FEW SAMPLES of the geology I have been describing in this book. I have chosen each of them to tell a story.

Photo 7.1: Flints

Photo 7.1 shows some typical forms that flints take. Starting from top left, what we see are:

◊ a carious flint – flints with internal cavities like this one are not rare in the UK but rare or even absent from some other areas where flints are found (e.g. the Caribbean)

◊ a burrow made by some deep-sea creature into which siliceous seafloor ooze flowed and crystallised: the burrow has now been cast as a flint

◊ a piece of a sheet flint – a continuous or semi-continuous layer of flint that filled a crack in chalk

◊ a tabular or semi-tabular flint – these are large, flattish flints that typically form courses between two layers of chalk *(see Photo 3.2)*

◊   a nodular flint – this might have filled part of a burrow, or simply formed in a bulge in the chalk: nodular flints often replace something else that was buried in the seafloor ooze but rotted or dissolved away, leaving a void, so they can be casts of something that, had it survived, might have been fossilised, and
◊   a piece of flint that has preserved some fossils both on its outer surface and within the black silica.

From the Cretaceous, we move to the Palæogene. Sarsen stones were described *in Chapter 4*, but (because I like it) I include another here as Photo 7.2. The surface shows the marks left by Palæogene raindrops falling on the dune this used to be, and tracks left by an insect in the sand that hardened to form this rock.

Photo 7.2: A piece of sarsen, found near Bucklebury Alley

The Bagshot sands were laid down between 34 million and 41 million years ago; while exposure to the air, the wind and rain, or to twenty-first-century feet or bicycles, can separate the grains, in other places time and pressure have bound them together quite tightly (and areas have cemented to form sandstone). Photo 7.3 shows a piece I pulled from the roots of a fallen tree near The Coombes *(see Appendix 4 for directions)* – this is not yet sandstone, but I might have to rub quite hard if I wanted to turn it back into loose sand.

The close-up shows quartz (sand) grains of several sizes packed tightly around a few tiny clasts (fragments of some stone) with gaps filled by yellow- and orange-stained ferriferous material. It would take a better microscope to determine whether this material is iron cement, or iron-stained clay or silt performing a similar function.

Photos 7.3 and 7.4: Bagshot sand, found at The Coombes

The final sample illustrates one resource that Iron Age smelters were looking for in river gravels (at Upper Bucklebury, for example: *see Photo 8.3*). Here are two flints, one nodular and the other a broken fragment, that have been coated with iron oxide. Between them I've placed a nodule of ironstone, of the kind found in river gravels and periglacial deposits. Iron minerals that formed where soil microbes instigated chemical reduction (siderite, for example) will dissolve in water. However, in mildly alkaline conditions (such as where that water has later dissolved chalk or other types of limestone) they oxidise and precipitate out. These can be visualised as successive stages of erosion: rain falls on areas rich in suitable minerals, some of which are dissolved or simply suspended. The solution subsequently flows to chalk/limestone areas, where the iron is precipitated.

Photo 7.5: Iron nodule and iron-coated flints

The nodule was found near Walbury Camp;
the flints were found at Winterbourne Chalk Pit SSSI

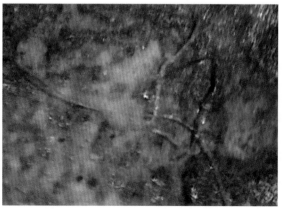

The close-up of the left-hand sample shows three thicknesses of iron (yellow staining, and orange crystals that darken the thicker the deposit) over a cast of roots or possibly a worm track preserved in the surface of the flint.

Photo 7.6: Close-up of left-hand iron-coated flint

8

Four walks round interesting places

ANY WALKS COULD EXPLORE Berkshire's geology and archæology; I've chosen these because they're circular, car parking is fairly straightforward, lunch can be found easily and they offer a range of options.

Where?	How long?	How hard? What shoes?	What will I see?	When's best?
Sulham	5¾ miles	Easy, level, trainers fine	Original course of Kennet, periglacial ground forms (possibly pingos)	Dry weather
Thatcham (loop)	4 miles	Easy, level, trainers fine	The Greenham scarp, water meadows, canal and railway	Dry, sunny weather
Thatcham (extension)	3½ miles	Moderate, steep, trainers fine	The Kennet valley, where Bronze Age settlements were found, original course of Kennet	Dry, sunny weather
Cookham Dean	4 miles	Moderate, mostly level, trainers fine	Thames river terraces, Seaford Nodular chalk	Winter, dry weather
Inkpen	8½ miles	Strenuous, steep, can be muddy, wear boots	Upper Greensand, chalk ridge and outcrops, Neolithic barrows, Iron Age 'hillfort'	Dry weather

Sulham: A river valley with no river

A LONG BUT EASY, 'there and back' walk through beautiful countryside that not many people visit.

Preparation: The walk is mostly on good surfaces; trainers should be fine unless the weather has been wet, but some paths can get overgrown so a stick (for thrashing down nettles) might be helpful. It can be muddy in places, so it is best to go in fine weather. The circuit is about five-and-three-quarter miles, but if you feel like a longer walk a detour through Moor Copse nature reserve is well worth it. The Greyhound in Tidmarsh does good lunches, but (especially at weekends) you may need to reserve.

Directions: North along A340 from A4; after crossing the M4, look for a small, discreet turning on the right; the car park is small and may be busy at weekends.

Take the pedestrian exit from the car park (not the one you drove into) and turn right. Cross the bridge over the Sulham Brook and turn left on to the byway. Follow it round the edge of Moor Copse nature reserve to a gate into the reserve; go through the gate and follow the path through the next two gates. At the corner of Horsemoor Wood the path forks: on the outward journey take the right-hand fork, through a gate to skirt the northern edge of the wood. You will cross Sulham Brook again.

This path joins another that bends right, to follow the eastern edge of the wood (outside it, this time). In front of you is the Sulham gap, carved by the Kennet and the proto-Pang; they used to flow through here to join the Thames near Pangbourne, but were both diverted (in different directions) during the Devensian glaciation: *see Chapter 5.* On the opposite bank (now Sulham Hill) you'll see the fine Georgian Sulham House; if you look in the direction we're walking, you'll see Wilder's Folly on a bare hill slightly to the west of the (wooded) river bank. After about half a mile you reach a path running across; turn right, over another bridge across the Sulham Brook and through a hazel coppice to a footbridge across the M4.

Once across follow the path through mixed broadleaf woodland, between Malpas and Pond Farms, to the road; keep going in the same direction, along the road, round an S-bend until you see a sign for another set of footpaths. Turn right on to the 'restricted byway' and follow it all the way to the M4, where you turn left through a gate. If you look south from anywhere along this path, you will see Hogmoor Field *(Photo 8.1)*: the field contains several dips, often filled with water. These are at least partly filled with peat, so are not recent: the Beenham Grange river terrace underlies the soil we can see; these might be the remains of pingos *(see Chapter 5)*.

Photo 8.1: Hogmoor Field

Retrace your steps. If you're feeling fit, when re-entering Horsemoor Wood the fork we did not take leads into Moor Copse, where several paths will lead you back to the car park, adding two or perhaps three miles to the walk, but through one of the most beautiful nature reserves in Berkshire.

Thatcham: The longest continuously inhabited settlement in the British Isles

A WALK IN TWO STAGES, from the 3rd millennium CE to the 500th millennium BCE and back; at times, if you use your imagination you will see pretty much what the first visitors to Berkshire saw.

Preparation: The walk is mostly on good surfaces; trainers should be fine. The first loop is about four miles (and involves crossing the railway); the second stage (there and back) about three-and-a-half miles and involves climbing then coming back down a steep hill. Both loops can be muddy in places, so it is best to go in fine weather. There are pubs, restaurants and two supermarkets in Thatcham, and a café at the Nature Discovery Centre.

Directions: As you approach Thatcham from the east along the A4, you will pass an old chapel. At the next traffic lights, turn left, and leave your car in the Pay and Display car park outside Waitrose.

First stage: loop

Leave the car park through the shopping arcade next to Waitrose. The market place (Thatcham Broadway) is probably fourteenth century, and a few seventeenth- or eighteenth-century buildings survive, including two coaching inns where the Broadway joins what used to be the Bath Road (now the A4). Cross the Broadway, turn right and then left into the High Street; at the far end turn into Church Lane, which will give a fair impression of Thatcham before the motor car. You will pass an attractive nineteenth-century United Reformed church before reaching St Mary's, which has a Norman south doorway, a thirteenth-century north arcade and a fifteenth-century tower. If the bellringers are at work, five of the bells you hear were cast in the seventeenth century.

Turn right and follow the path round the churchyard, till you reach Church Gate; turn right again and follow the road past the roundabout. Cross it and head diagonally (south-west) across the playing field, to a gateway halfway along the boundary hedge. Cross the lane into the farmer's field which (at the time of writing) is a surviving example of a medieval water meadow. Follow the line of trees until you reach a break, then turn left into the Nature Discovery Centre, passing through the community orchard and heading for the lake. The lakes here are former pits that took gravel from the Beenham Grange river terrace (Devensian: *see Chapter 5*). Follow the lake round (café and toilets are to your right; both ways round are attractive) and at the south-west corner cross the track and follow the public footpath through the overspill car park (you should now be heading almost due west, and roughly parallel to the railway line).

Once past the first car park (there is a second, further along) you start to see ponds, reedbeds and fringing willow and alder scrub. This is the Thatcham Reedbeds and, if you can ignore the twentieth- and twenty-first-century civic detritus (fences, made paths, power lines) you are looking at a landscape not vastly unlike what Mesolithic visitors to Thatcham saw. This is a river meadow (hamm) growing reed (thatch) and this is probably how the settlement got its name. To your right, in the sewage works, evidence of a middle Stone Age (Mesolithic) settlement was found; the site may have been occupied for several centuries.

Carry on past the reedbeds (ignore the left turn just before the second overspill car park). If you are here in June or July, take time to look through the scrub on the southern (reedbed) side of the car park: pyramidal orchids occasionally come up here. When you reach the stream, turn left over the footbridge, keeping your eyes and ears open for rare wetland birds. Eventually you will reach an area of willow carr, with an embankment in front of you: this is where the Lambourn (which at this point is flowing above the level of the reedbeds) joins the Kennet. In prehistory river junctions were often regarded as sacred places, and that might be why our distant ancestors decided to settle here.

Photo 8.2: Thatcham reedbeds

At this point we zoom forward in time. In front of you is a stretch of the river Kennet, absorbed into the Kennet and Avon Canal in the late eighteenth century CE, and as we turn left on to the towpath we pass under Brunel's Great Western Railway (1830s). Once past the railway, the view opens out across fields that were probably water meadows in the Tudor period to the ridge of Greenham and Crookham Commons. The Kennet may have flowed up there before the Anglian ice age: the ridge is largely the Silchester river terrace (late Anglian: *see Chapter 5*) above Thames Group London clay and Harwich Formation sand *(see Chapter 4)*, and Palæolithic remains have been found on both commons. On the scarp facing us we see Bowdown Woods.

Follow the towpath to Widmead Lock, then turn back towards Thatcham (north-west). This track can be muddy, and floods in very wet weather. When you reach the railway, there are lights but they are there for engine drivers, not for you, so be careful! The track will lead you back to the first overspill car park *(see above)*;

retrace your steps to St Mary's church. Go through the churchyard to admire the church and its flint walls. As you leave the churchyard there are attractive old houses on both sides of the street. Cross the Broadway and return to your car.

Second stage: there and back

Leave the car park from the corner opposite Waitrose; at the traffic lights, cross to the north side of the A4. You will see some attractive old half-timbered buildings, dating back to the days of the Bath Road. Take the first left on to Park Avenue (after A-Plan Insurance), cross the road and take Hartley Way (between the houses) to the green. Follow the path diagonally across the green, then Vincent Road out to Hart's Hill Road, and over at the zebra crossing. Turn left and head towards the hill; as you reach a gate that leads into a meadow on your right, look diagonally across to Dunston Park. Postholes for both Bronze Age and Iron Age houses were found when the estate was being built.

Pass through the gate into the meadow and follow the path diagonally across to a very muddy patch by a footbridge. Cross the bridge and turn left, then follow Simmons Field as it winds, first right and then left, twice, to Floral Way (the main Thatcham bypass). Taking care (people drive quickly along Floral Way) cross to a footpath into the fields. The actual footpath runs left, then right, round the edge of the field, but the farmer may have allowed a path to cut the corner. Follow the steep path to the houses on the first ridge, then stop to catch your breath and turn round to enjoy the view for almost ten miles in each direction, along the Kennet Valley. Looking east, you should also be able to see, on the far side of the Greenham/Crookham ridge, the valley of the Enborne as it flows past the south side of that ridge to join the Kennet near Aldermaston.

Keep following the path, round then between the houses, across a drive and up a little further into another field, offering even better views. Taking the left-hand path, keep your eye on the gravel pit across the road (this may be easier to see in winter). A Bronze

Age settlement and cemetery were found here, but much more excitingly, evidence of iron working dated to around 1000 BCE: this is the oldest iron-working site known in southern England, and after it was found the start date for the Iron Age in Britain had to be pushed back 250 years! The pit is working the Bucklebury Common river terrace (Cromerian: *see Chapter 5*): the Kennet flowed through here from Cold Ash (west-north-west of this spot) before being pushed south to its present course during the Anglian stage. Ironstone nodules, and flints encrusted with iron, can be found in these gravels.

Photo 8.3: Hart's Hill Quarry: Bagshot sand, Bucklebury Common gravel and the earliest iron-working site in Britain

Heading back down Hart's Hill, at the playing field we carry on to the old yellow-washed chapel. This was the Chapel of St Thomas à Becket, built around 1304 CE (a fair in honour of that saint used to be held in Thatcham every year). The chapel became a school in 1707 (and is now known as the Old Bluecoat School).

Cross the A4 at the traffic lights, and return to your car.

Cookham Dean: River terraces and chalk

A CIRCULAR WALK, showing how much material the Thames removed after it was diverted during the Anglian stage, and an interesting chalk pit.

Preparation: The walk is mostly on good surfaces; trainers should be fine unless the weather has been wet; but the surface in the chalk pit is poor and it was quite overgrown when I visited it. The circuit is about four miles. It can be muddy in places, so it is best to go in fine weather, after the leaves have fallen. There are two pubs in Cookham Dean, but (especially at weekends) you may need to reserve for lunch.

Directions: North along A404 from M4 junction; south on to A308 at roundabout just before M40; from Pinkneys Green, follow signposts to Winterhill. At Bisham Wood look for on-road parking; this may be busy at weekends.

First stage: Thames terraces

Wherever you park, once in the wood look for the light where the scarp falls away (north) and head in that direction. You will find a path heading west (to your left) along the front of the ridge. Outcropping at several points we find the Gerrard's Cross river terrace (Cromerian: see Chapter 5). Among the expected flints it contains well-rounded pebbles of quartz (obvious), quartzite (typically a sandy brown, smooth and hard) and occasional igneous and other pebbles brought down from Wales and the Midlands in Northern Drift (See Chapter 5). Fossils can be found in this gravel.

After about half a mile we reach a spot with a bench offering an excellent view across the valley to All Saints Church, Marlow. On the far side of the river you should be able to pick out the corresponding Gerrard's Cross terrace above the town, as well as the Winter Hill (Anglian) terrace below it and, on our side of the river, the Shepperton terrace (Devensian). *Photos 5.2 and 5.3 may help.*

Retracing your steps, you should eventually see a narrow path to your left; it does not matter if you miss this, as either path will do. When you reach Quarry Wood Road, cross (carefully! the road is steep and bendy, so drivers have little time to see you and brake) and take the public footpath signposted opposite. This winds up and down for about half a mile, the scarp falling steeply to your left and the wood changing from classic Chilterns beechwood to a mixture with yew, hazel and holly prominent. Eventually you reach a driveway, with two paths opposite: the left-hand path goes down into the woods if you would like to explore them further, and the right-hand path (waymarked) takes us to the Winter Hill viewpoint. There are excellent views from several places along the open ground, but the best are probably from the bench where the path brings us out.

Second stage: Cretaceous and Quaternary

Turning south (away from the river), cross the road and head off down Startins Lane. Take the first public footpath on the right, and as it descends note the Lambeth Group sands revealed in the banks. At the road, turn left then right into King's Lane. When you reach the green, take the path up to your left: you will see the Cookham Dean chalk pit in front of you. There are various paths into the pit, but watch your footing. This is a fairly unusual outcrop of Seaford chalk, with several bands of both tabular and nodular flint in the face, an interesting fault and periglacial solution features (cracks and pipes filled with Lambeth Group sands and clays).

Returning to the path and turning right, climb the hill, noting the gravels and substantial flints in the path and verges. When you reach the green, turn right for the Mole and Badger pub. If you do not fancy this one, a footpath runs to the right across the front of the pub and after five minutes or so you will see a sign to the Jolly Farmer.

The path turns right, through a gate and down through King's Coppice Farm. If you visit before Christmas, you might see some of the turkeys they raise. The path runs down to a farm road, crosses it and carries on slightly upwards to a gate on to Grubwood Lane. If you cross the lane, and scramble up the bank, you will be back in Quarry Wood (aka Bisham Wood) and a right turn along the path will lead you back to your car.

Inkpen: The highest point in Berkshire

A LONG, STRENUOUS WALK; but you'll pass the oldest rocks visible at the surface in Berkshire and a magnificent hillfort, and on a fine day the views are stupendous.

Preparation: The hill is very steep; wear good boots and consider bringing a stick. Some stages involve road walking. The paths can be muddy, so it is best to go in fine weather. There is a pub in Inkpen (the Crown and Garter), and a footpath apparently runs from the Combe Gibbet car park to it, but I have not been able to check.

Parking: A4 to Lower Denford (just east of Hungerford); follow signs for Inkpen; at the crossroad after The Swan (now closed), turn right and immediately left. This (narrow, windy) road will take you to the Combe Gibbet car park; you could leave your car here and modify the instructions that follow, or turn left past it, drive past the northern bank of Walbury Hillfort, turn left at the T-junction (signposted Faccombe and Ashmansworth) and park at the Walbury Hill car park.

This path is good at any time of year (in dry weather); the geology may be easier to appreciate in winter (Bungum Lane, in particular, can get quite overgrown).

Take the byway out of the car park's north-west corner, and follow it towards Combe Gibbet. As you walk, look at the path surface; iron nodules can fairly often be found. Soon, you will pass through the outer bank of the hillfort. This is all that is left; and it is on private land so an Ordnance Survey map may be helpful to appreciate just how large it was. This is the highest point in Berkshire and the view to your right will tell you why the hillfort was built here.

In a bit less than a mile you reach the Combe Gibbet car park, where you cross the road and continue along the byway towards the Gibbet. The original (a replacement is here now) was built in 1676 on top of a long barrow, to execute a pair of adulterers for murdering the man's wife and son.

Photo 8.4: Combe Gibbet, from Walbury Hillfort

After the Gibbet, carry on along the byway, which soon dips and is joined by a path from the south. About 75metres past that junction, turn right through a gate, pass across a thicket to another gate, where you turn back towards the Gibbet (you'll see a path in the grass) for about 50metres. Look for where it is joined by a path heading north (sharply downhill). Soon this bends right, towards a copse, carrying on down the front of Inkpen Hill. Follow the path round the edge of the copse then take a left turn going sharply down to a gate.

Through the gate, descend through a plantation (the path can get quite overgrown, so long trousers and a stick or secateurs are sensible). It joins a field boundary. When you emerge from the copse, a path is running across the track you are on; turn left. After a while you may start to notice sandstone pebbles and ironstone nodules appearing in the path. This is the Upper Greensand, the oldest exposed rock in Berkshire *(see Photo 3.1)*.

When you reach a gate (marked 'Private'), turn right (there is a signpost, but when last I was here it was quite overgrown). Look to your right: in a few yards you should see a sandstone boulder in the bushes. This track (which widens and turns into a green lane) is Bungum Lane. Occasional sandstone pebbles, cobbles (and at the lower end, even small boulders) are all that can be seen in the path surface, but if it has recently rained and you are naughty enough to cut across to the (private) farm track, more evidence of the Greensand can be seen. At the lower end, it is worth peering into the ditch running along the path.

When you reach the road (hello, John and Jenny!) turn right. Just before the village sign, turn right again up a farm track (you do have right of way) and through the gate at the end. Follow the path back up Inkpen Hill; if you scan its surface you will see the usual chalk and flint mixture; although this is only about 100metres east of Bungum Lane, there is little or no sign of the Upper Greensand. At the copse, you rejoin the path you took down; it is a steep and challenging climb, but the views are stupendous (as are the wildflowers and orchids, in summer).

At the top, instead of rejoining the byway turn left and follow the path that runs parallel to it and, eventually, across the northern front of the barrow the Gibbet is built on. This will give you some idea of the scale of the barrow (which is not so obvious from the other side). From here, you have a good view of one corner of the Walbury Hillfort earthwork. Rejoin the byway and retrace your steps to your car.

Photo 8.5: Walbury Hillfort, from Combe Gibbet

Appendix One

What may have shaped Planet Earth

AS OUTLINED IN THE INTRODUCTION, the theory of plate tectonics Explains the make-up of the **bedrock** and **superficial deposits** that provide the structure of Berkshire.

The Earth's four concentric layers are: a crust, which varies in thickness; a solid mantle that is approximately 2,900km thick; an outer core about 2,100km thick that is liquid and mainly iron and nickel (some lighter elements may also be present); and an inner core of the same materials, that is solid and roughly two-thirds the size of the Moon. Our planet's radius is roughly 6,370km.

While the average thickness of the Earth's crust is probably around 20km, it is much thinner under the oceans (on average, around 7km); and while the continents average about 33km in thickness some areas of them are much thinner than this, and some much thicker. It may be around 80km from the top of Mount Everest to the base of the crust beneath the Himalayas.

The base of the crust is not flat: broadly, if there is a mountain above ground (or on the ocean floor) the crust will bulge below ground (below the ocean floor). In rift valleys (or ocean trenches), for example, the crust is thin both above and below ground (ocean floor). *Figure A1.1 shows what this looks like.* The crust rests on the mantle, so the mantle is much closer to ground level where the crust is thin, and may even break through it (as some types of volcano do).

The crust and the top 100km or so of the mantle together form the **lithosphere**. The lithosphere operates in many ways as a unit, and both are mainly made up of silicate minerals; but the crust is mainly *low-density* silicates, with plenty of aluminium and potassium, while the mantle is mainly *high-density* silicates, containing more magnesium and iron. Rocks nearer the surface are cooler than the rocks below them and, as depth increases, so does pressure from the rocks above. The lithosphere forms fourteen major plates (and a large number of microplates) that move slowly past, over or under one another, causing oceans to open and close, continents to form and break up, mountains to rise and the floors of rifts to fall. They can move because gradually local heat and pressure cause rigid mantle to become **asthenosphere** (the next 300km or so of the mantle), which is ductile – though solid, the rocks that make it up deform more easily than the cooler rocks above them. Sometimes this deformation is a kind of flow (over long periods the rocks change shape) and at other times it happens violently (when rocks break).

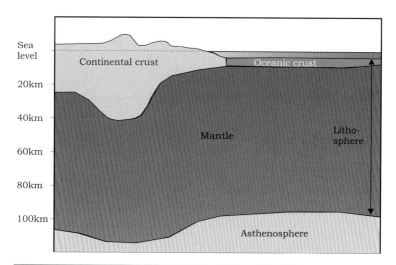

Figure A1.1: Crust, lithosphere and asthenosphere
Redrawn by author from Park, 2012

Several factors working together are believed to cause the movement of the plates that make up the lithosphere. One is heat: where it can, hotter matter will rise and cooler matter will sink.

Another is gravity: denser matter will sink beneath less dense matter unless something prevents this. These two are related: as matter heats up it expands, causing its density to reduce; conversely, as it cools it shrinks, becoming denser. So, as hotter rock expands it seeks to rise (through gaps or cracks or simply by pushing other rocks aside) and when it does rise cooler, denser rock can sink behind it, a slow process of *solid-state convection* that we believe is constantly occurring in the mantle. Rock is a poor conductor of heat, meaning that once hot it stays hot for a very long time; so, although rock cools as it rises, the cooling is slow, and the rising rock often stays hotter than the surrounding rock. Conversely, as sinking rock moves nearer to the core it gains heat, but this too will be slow and the falling rock stays cooler (and therefore denser) than the surrounding mantle for a long time. Moreover, the deeper it goes, the higher the pressure on it from all the rocks above, which tends to prevent expansion. If the rock were to melt it might flow more easily, but rock (like most materials) expands when it melts – so by restricting it from expanding, pressure also restricts its ability to melt, meaning that rocks at depth may remain solid at temperatures far higher than what we think of as their melting point.

Now, if rocks break, hot rock under pressure below them may rise by pushing through the gap. Where this happens quickly the release of pressure can allow the melting that was constrained to now take place, and this, too, can help rock masses to push past one another; but this does not need to happen. Gravity (i.e. relative density) may be the most important factor driving some rocks upwards and others downwards.

There are three main tectonic processes: rifting and spreading, **subduction** and parallel movement. These are usually defined by describing how the plates move. **Constructive** movement sees two plates draw apart, opening a rift between them and drawing magma up into the rift), **destructive** movement sees one plate subducted beneath another and **conservative** movement sees one plate slide past another. It is easiest to explain constructive movement first, then conservative movement and destructive movement last.

Constructive plate boundaries

Figure A1.2 shows a **constructive boundary** beneath an ocean; as the plates move apart, new rock rising between them from the asthenosphere erupts as an undersea volcano, adding a 'push' to the already-moving plates, and pouring out lava that will cool and form new oceanic crust.

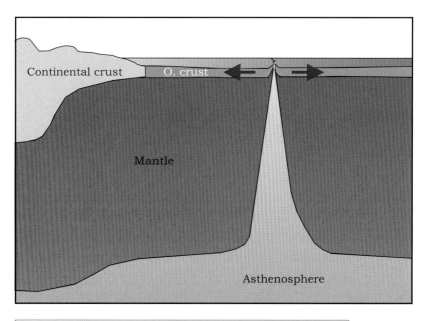

Figure A1.2: A constructive boundary opening up an ocean
Redrawn by author from Park, 2012

This happens in several stages. First, gravity or convection starts to draw two plates apart. This stretches the mantle and the oceanic crust above it (the lithosphere), drawing hot rock up. Since this hot rock is less dense than the surrounding lithosphere, it is more buoyant, causing the oceanic crust above it to bulge. Figure A1.2 shows this as a point, with an undersea volcano breaking through the middle; but it is more like a boundary between two plates with these eruptions happening all along the boundary.

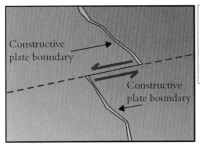

Figure A1.3: Transcurrent fault offsetting a constructive boundary

Redrawn by author from Rothery, 2017

Many **transcurrent** (or 'transform') **faults** form across the boundary – 'transcurrent' describes parallel movement in opposite directions. The faults relieve the stress along the boundary, and can also have the effect of moving it, for example to go round a stronger area of rock: effectively, introducing a zig-zag. In Figure A1.3 the red arrows show the direction in which each side of the constructive boundary is moving, and thus the direction of movement along the fault, and the dotted lines show how the fault continues past the boundary to help relieve stress.

As well as across boundaries, faults can form across earlier faults, effectively creating networks of parallel faults. Eventually, **graben** can form – an area of rock sinks between two parallel splits, like a wedge falling into the gap – or **horsts** – where parallel

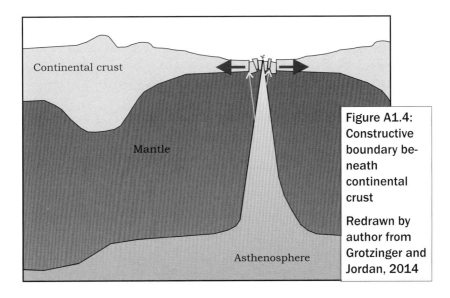

Figure A1.4: Constructive boundary beneath continental crust

Redrawn by author from Grotzinger and Jordan, 2014

splitting pushes areas of rock upwards. Ultimately, rift valleys develop (very large graben, or several smaller graben joining up). Such splits offer channels for magma to escape (if very buoyant, it might simply push its way through, causing the split). Figure A1.4 shows three parallel graben, separated by horsts, with the central graben being widened by a volcano. Rift valleys on land tend to be surrounded by volcanoes; as well as the central channel in Figure A1.4, magma might force its way through other splits (indicated by the yellow arrows in the figure). Rift valleys can flood, and it is believed that new oceans begin this way: the Red Sea is an example.

Conservative plate boundaries

Where gravity or convection drags plates in parallel but opposite directions, they scrape past one another doing little damage to each other – while still parallel. In Figure A1.3, for example, the transcurrent fault forms a **conservative boundary** where it runs between the two constructive plate boundaries.

Figure A1.5 shows what happens when conservative boundaries change direction (this can happen, for example, to get round outcrops of more resistant rock). One change can open a constructive boundary (pulling the two plates apart) and another can create a destructive one *(see next subsection for details)*. Figure A1.5 illustrates what may be happening simultaneously in many places along

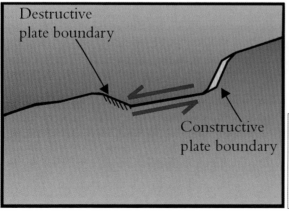

Destructive plate boundary

Constructive plate boundary

Figure A1.5: Conservative boundary

Redrawn by author from Rothery, 2017

a conservative plate boundary. Because of this, movement along conservative boundaries is not smooth and continuous but jerky and sudden: when sufficient force has built up, a section will move, causing the earth to 'quake'. For this reason, earthquakes are found on either side of the boundary; sometimes volcanoes are, too.

Destructive plate boundaries

Where gravity or convection drags plates towards each other, the lighter passes over the heavier, which is subducted back into the mantle. Where an oceanic plate is subducted beneath another *(see Figure A1.6)*, or beneath a continental plate, a trench forms at the junction and the uppermost plate crumples and throws up mountains. As the figure shows, such mountains are often volcanic: one plate scraping beneath the other can trigger earthquakes, opening faults through which magma may rise (driven by relative buoyancy). Moreover, subduction brings very high pressure, which can drive magma upwards.

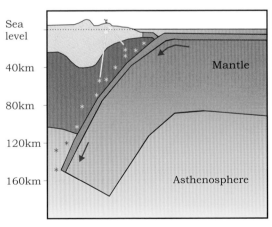

Figure A1.6: Destructive plate boundary

Redrawn by author from Rothery, 2017

Where two continental plates converge, denser oceanic lithosphere will usually be subducted beneath the less dense continental crust; eventually, two pieces of continental crust (opposite shores of the ocean, say) may crash into one another and fuse together *(see Figure A1.7)*. While the oceanic lithosphere

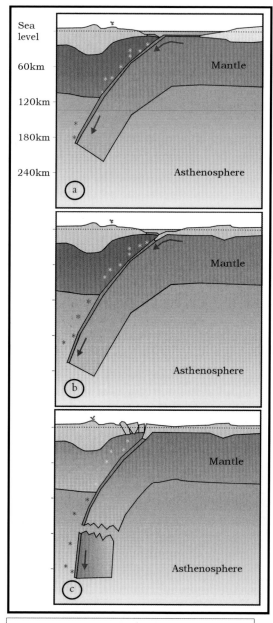

continues   denser and   cooler   than the   surrounding asthenosphere, it may continue to subduct and eventually break off, another potential cause of earthquakes.

Continental drift; oceans

Figure   A1.2 showed how continents can be pushed apart, or break up,   as   constructive boundaries   open; this   process   can be   enhanced   by c o n s e r v a t i v e boundaries   (for example,   northward movement   along   the San Andreas fault has opened up the Gulf of   California);   and Figure   A1.7   shows how   **destructive boundaries**   can draw   continents together   and   fuse them.   Constructive boundaries   are constantly   opening oceans   and   creating

Figure A1.7: Destructive boundary between continental plates

Redrawn by author from Rothery, 2017

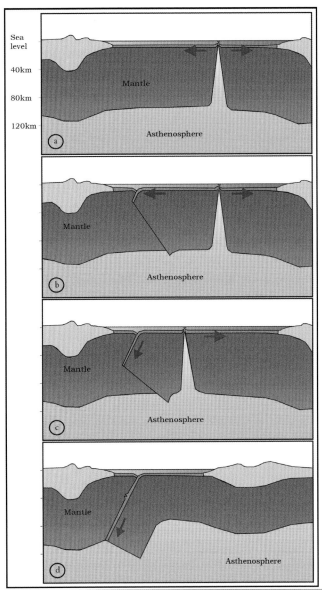

new ocean floor, while destructive boundaries are closing them and recycling old crust. It is believed that there is no area of ocean crust more than 240 million years old. Figure A1.8 summarises these processes: (a) shows a new ocean opening, rather as the Atlantic is doing today, (b) shows a constructive boundary still opening the ocean, but one side beginning to subduct beneath a continental plate, (c) shows gravity dragging the

Figure A1.8: Stages in the life of an ocean

Redrawn by author from Rothery, 2017 and Park, 2012

subducting plate down faster than the constructive boundary can generate new ocean floor, rather as the Pacific is doing (except that the Pacific is subducting on all sides), while in (d) the ocean has closed so far that the constructive boundary itself has been subducted. Eventually, oceans can close and the continents on either side of them fuse together.

Faults

A fault is a place where the rock has broken and one or both sides of the break have moved. I explained transcurrent faults in describing constructive plate boundaries *(see Figure A1.3)*; the two other types are **normal faults** (where the rock on one side of the fault has fallen: the graben that I mentioned are often surrounded by normal faults) and **reverse faults** (where one side has been pushed upwards: a horst is an example of this).

Appendix Two

Geological time

IT IS CURRENTLY BELIEVED that the Earth has existed for about 4,600 million years (Ma). Geologists use a division that is simple in outline – **eons** are made up of **eras**, that are made up of **periods**, that in turn are made up of **epochs**. However, some widely recognised subdivisions have not been formally included (so are not, strictly speaking, eras or periods) and occasionally different names are used for different aspects of the same thing:

Age (Ma):	Eons:	Eras:		Periods:	Began (Ma):	Epochs:
				Quaternary		Holocene
					2.6	Pleistocene
				Neogene		Pliocene
		CENOZOIC	Tertiary		23	Miocene
				Palæogene		Oligocene
						Eocene
66	PHANEROZOIC (continues overleaf)				66	Palæocene
				Cretaceous		Upper
					145	Lower
		MESOZOIC		Jurassic		Upper
						Middle
					201	Lower
				Triassic		Upper
						Middle
252					252	Lower

(table continues overleaf)

Age (Ma):	Eons:	Eras:		Periods:	Began (Ma):	Epochs:
			Upper	Permian	299	Upper
						Lower
				Carboniferous		Stephanian
						West-phalian
						Namurian
					359	Dinantian
				Devonian		Upper
						Middle
419	PHANEROZOIC	PALÆOZOIC			419	Lower
			Lower	Silurian		Pridoli
						Ludlow
						Wenlock
					444	Llandovery
				Ordovician		Ashgill
						Caradoc
						Llandeilo
						Llanvirn
						Arenig
					485	Tremadoc
				Cambrian		Merioneth
						St David's
541					541	Caerfai
1,000	PROTE-ROZOIC	Late				
1,600		Mid-				
2,500		Early				
1,000	ARCHÆAN	Neo-				
1,000		Meso-				
1,000		Eo-				
1,000	HADEAN					

All rocks older than Phanerozoic are known as Precambrian. The suffix –zoic relates to life; the prefixes phanero- and protero- mean 'visible, evident' and 'former, earlier'; and the prefixes palæo-, eo-, meso-, ceno- and neo- mean 'ancient', 'old', 'middle', 'recent' and 'new' respectively. The suffix –gene means 'born'; the suffix –cene is a different form of the word ceno-, so means 'recent': thus palæocene is the oldest part of the most recent ('cenozoic') era.

The Cretaceous, Tertiary and Quaternary periods are well represented in Berkshire, and can be divided into **ages** and (in some cases) sub-ages:

Eras:	Periods:	Epochs:	Began (Ma):	Ages:	Sub-ages:
CENOZOIC (continues overleaf)	Quaternary	Holo-cene	0.004	Meghalayan	
			0.008	Northgrippian	
			0.012	Greenlandian	
		Pleistocene	0.1	Tarantian	Devensian[G] Ipswichian
			0.8	Ionian/ Chibanian (1)	Wolstonian[G] Hoxnian Anglian[G] Cromerian
			1.8	Calabrian	Beestonian[G] Pastonian
			2.6	Gelasian	Baventian[G] Bramertonian Antian Thurnian Ludhamian Waltonian

(table continues overleaf)

Eras:	Periods:		Epochs:	Began (Ma):	Ages:	Sub-ages:
CENOZOIC	Tertiary	Neogene	Plio-cene	3.6	Piacenzian	
				5.3	Zanclean	
			Miocene	7	Messinian	
				12	Tortonian	
				14	Serravallian	
				16	Langhian	
				20	Burdigalian	
				23	Aquitanian	
		Palæogene	Oligo-cene	28	Chattian	
				34	Rupelian	
			Eocene	38	Priabonian	
				41	Bartonian	
				48	Lutetian	
				56	Ypresian	
			Palæo-cene	59	Thanetian	
				62	Selandian	
				66	Danian	

Eras:	Periods:	Epochs:	Began (Ma):	Ages:	Sub-ages:
MESOZOIC	Cretaceous	Upper	72	Maastrichtian	Upper Lower
			84	Campanian	Upper Middle Lower
			86	Santonian	Upper Middle Lower
			90	Coniacian	Upper Middle Lower
			94	Turonian	Upper Middle Lower
			101	Cenomanian	
		Lower	113	Albian	Upper Middle Lower
			125	Aptian	Clansayesian Gargasian Bedoulian
			129	Barremian	Upper Lower
			133	Hauterivian	
			140	Valanginian	Upper Lower
			145	Berriasian	
NOTES:	(1) The Ionian and, more recently, the Chibanian have been proposed as alternative names for the middle Pleistocene.				
	(2) In the table, G denotes a glacial sub-age, or a sub-age with alternating glacial and interglacial phases.				

The present, Holocene, epoch has lasted 10,000 years; the present, Meghalayan age has lasted 4,200 years and began with a 200-year drought that affected key early human civilisations from Greece to China, a point that more of us should bear in mind. Human archæological remains that have been found in Berkshire can be placed in geological context as follows:

Age (Ka):	Ep.:	Ages (geol.):	Sub-ages (geol.):	Ages (human):	Tool-styles (human):	Dated to (Ka):
4	Holocene	North-grippian		Neolithic	Neolithic	4–5.5
8	Holocene	Green-landian		Mesolithic	Mesolithic	4–5.5
12	Pleistocene	Taran-tian	Deven-sian	Palæo-lithic	Mousterian (1)	100–150
110	Pleistocene	Taran-tian	Ips-wichian	Palæo-lithic	None yet found	None yet found
130	Pleistocene	Ionian/Chiban-ian	Wol-stonian	Palæo-lithic	Levallois	100–250
352	Pleistocene	Ionian/Chiban-ian	Hoxni-an	Palæo-lithic	Acheulian Clactonian (2)	430–50
424	Pleistocene		Anglian	Palæo-lithic	Acheulian Clactonian (2)	430–50
NOTES:	(1) When these techniques were used in what is now the UK is no guide to when they were used elsewhere in the world.					
	(2) The Acheulian and Clactonian styles may have overlapped (or been used at the same time).					
	(3) This table is amplified in Appendix Three.					

Appendix Three

Archæological sites and exhibits

IN BERKSHIRE, archæological sites are often on private land or hidden in woodland: the Megalithic Portal website at www.megalithic.co.uk/ provides directions to many (and some descriptions). Here I list a few that most people should find worth visiting, and some museums that exhibit Berkshire archæology. The second and third tables summarise what has been found in Berkshire: readers interested in the detail may wish to consult Oxford Archæology's 'Solent Thames Research Framework', available online at https://oxfordarchaeology.com/research-publication/solent-thames-research-framework/county-assessments, or Historic England's 'Heritage Gateway' at www.heritagegateway.org.uk/gateway/.

For convenience, I record sites west to east (not by date, 'importance' or any other criterion). Also, (for reasons geologists will appreciate) the oldest sites are in the bottom row of each table.

Where?	What?	Directions	Notes
Archæological sites			
Donnington Castle	14th-century castle, much knocked-about in Civil War	West along A4 from Newbury; at roundabout, north on to B4494; at mini-roundabout, west on to Grove Road and look for sign to right	English Heritage site; pay-and-display parking; free entry

Where?	What?	Directions	Notes
Windsor Castle	14th-century castle (on older foundations)	See Appendix 4	Castle worth a visit (but expensive); walk round the castle and through Home Park offers good views
Silchester	Roman town walls and amphitheatre; English Heritage booklet worth acquiring before you go	West along A4 from Reading; south through Aldermaston to Baughurst; east towards Silchester; east on to Kings Road; east again on to Wall Lane; car park is on your right	Technically in Hampshire; English Heritage site; pay-and-display parking; free entry
Walbury Camp and Combe Gibbet	Ramparts of a 'hillfort', a long barrow and fantastic views	See Chapter 8	Walk in Chapter 8 is strenuous, but a stroll along the ridge is not
Lambourn Seven Barrows	A lovely, small nature reserve containing 26 barrows of various types (more nearby)	See Appendix 4	Limited parking
Archæological exhibits			
Hungerford Virtual Museum	Exhibits include a report on a Roman villa	www.hungerfordvirtualmuseum.co.uk/	Worth a look

Where?	What?	Directions	Notes
West Berkshire Museum	Small museum in 17th-century cloth hall; some prehistoric and more medieval, Tudor and recent exhibits	From the A4, take the A339 south; right at first roundabout; right at mini-roundabout; park at pay-and-display car park outside library	Museum is across from car park; free entry
Reading Museum	Extensive prehistoric, Roman and medieval collections	Use the Park and Ride service; take a bus to Reading Station	From the station, walk south along Blagrave Street; museum is on your left; free entry
Museum of English Rural Life, Reading	Strong on 18th to 20th centuries	From the M4, take the A33 north; at fork, east on Queen's Road; park in the multistorey car park	Turn left on to Queen's Road, cross at lights; walk south along Wellington Street; cross London Road and continue south along Redlands Road; museum is on your right; free entry
Maidenhead Heritage Centre	Strong on 20th century (a Spitfire simulator!), some prehistoric and Roman exhibits	From the M4, take the A308 into the town; at the first roundabout, east on Stafferton Way; park in the multistorey car park	Walk back out to A308, turn right (over the railway), right into Queen Street, right into York Road and left into Park Street; museum is on your left; free entry

APPENDIX THREE: Archæological sites and exhibits

The next table covers the Stone and Bronze Ages. It includes major sites only; the 'favour' column in the first table records a period before settlement began but for which there is evidence that proto-humans favoured particular *sites* over long periods (not just *areas*, such as Caversham). Dates show number of years 'before the present' (BP) and relate to the rightmost column in which entries appear (to record new developments during the period, and to keep the tables a manageable size). So, the Neolithic dates relate to sites where evidence of buildings was found, not the 'favour' or 'artefact' sites.

Sub-ages (geological):	Ages (human):	Artefacts:	Found: Favour:	Buildings:	Hamlets:	Dated to (,000 yrs BP):
	Late Bronze Age		Note 10	Reading, Maidenhead, Eton, Runnymede, Slough (note 11)	Thatcham, Burghfield (note 11)	3.0, 2.7–3.0
Northgrippian	Early, Middle Bronze Age			Lambourn, Burghfield, Reading, Bray		3.5–3.9, 3.5–3.8, 3.4–3.7, 3.0–3.6
	Neolithic	Burghfield	Kintbury, Thatcham	Lambourn, Burghfield, Eton, Runnymede, Horton (note 9)		5.3–5.8, 5.0–5.9, 5.3–5.6, 4.8–5.9, 4.8–5.3

| Sub-ages (geological): | Ages (human): | Found: | | | | Dated to (,000 yrs BP): |
		Artefacts:	Favour:	Buildings:	Hamlets:	
Greenlandian	Mesolithic (note 6)	Windsor (note 7)	Kintbury, Newbury (note 8)	Kintbury, Thatcham, Reading		7.9–10.2, 5.8–6.4, ?
Devensian		Maidenhead, Taplow (note 5)				100–150
Wolstonian (note 4)		Sonning, Woodley, Twyford				100–190
Hoxnian (note 4)		Reading, Remenham, Ruscombe, Cookham, Maidenhead, Slough				300–340
		Caversham (note 3)				370–420
Anglian (continued overleaf)	Paleolithic (continued overleaf)	Caversham, Emmer Green				430–450 (note1)

APPENDIX THREE: Archæological sites and exhibits

Sub-ages (geological):	Ages (human):	Found:				Dated to (,000 yrs BP):
		Artefacts:	Favour:	Buildings:	Hamlets:	
Anglian	Palæolithic (note 2)	Hamstead Marshall, Wash Common, Greenham, Brimpton				430–450 (note 1)

NOTES:

(1) Archaeologists believe the Caversham and Emmer Green sites are later than the others.

(2) Lower and Middle Palaeolithic artefacts are often found where they were dropped, or where rivers carried them – which may not be where they were used.

(3) There have been many (and extensive) finds in and around Caversham covering several periods without evidence of 'favour'.

(4) Assignment of artefacts to these sub-ages has been based on the tool-styles used (see Appendix 2), but where dated the date-ranges fit the timescales now accepted for these sub-ages quite badly (especially the 'Hoxnian' artefacts). In addition, single or small finds in clay-with-flints between Basildon and Pangbourne, between Hungerford and Newbury, and near Wokingham, may be Hoxnian or Wolstonian.

(5) Possibly also Sulhampstead.

(6) 'A significant concentration' (Chisham, 2006) of sites spread along the Kennet between Thatcham and Hungerford during the Early Mesolithic.

(7) Artefacts (sometimes single, sometimes many) have also been found in the Lambourn valley, and at Hungerford, Marsh Benham, Midgham, Ufton Green, Reading, Binfield, Wokingham, Earley, Bray, Holyport and Waltham St Lawrence, mostly undated.

Sub-ages (geological):	Ages (human):	Found:				Dated to (,000 yrs BP):
		Artefacts:	Favour:	Buildings:	Hamlets:	
NOTES:		(8) Kintbury site dated to between 9,100 and 11,300 BP, Newbury site to between 9,600 and 10,300 BP.				
		(9) With the exception of Horton (near Slough) (and possibly Runnymede), these appear to be monumental, not residential.				
		(10) Land boundaries (linear ditches and cross-ridge dykes in the Berkshire Downs) also appear in the Late Bronze Age.				
		(11) Trading centres found at Runnymede (single settlement) and Burghfield (hamlet).				

The following table covers the Iron Age and subsequent archæology. Because far more sites exist and because I want to record how human occupation of Berkshire developed this records 'first evidence' of e.g. villages, towns that continue to the present.

Ages (human):	Found:					
	Fields, farms (1):	Villages:	Towns:	Forts, castles (2):	Industry:	Other:
Tudor and Stuart		Shaw, East Ilsley, Greenham			Wokingham	
Medieval			Newbury, Woking-ham			Newbury, Ashampstead, Maidenhead, Slough (10)

APPENDIX THREE: Archæological sites and exhibits

Ages (human):	Found:					
	Fields, farms (1):	Villages:	Towns:	Forts, castles (2):	Industry:	Other:
Norman			Hunger-ford, (New) Windsor	Hamstead Marshall, Newbury, Windsor		Reading, Sonning (11)
Anglo-Saxon	Chieveley	Kintbury, Wickham, Beedon, Brightwalton, Boxford, Speen, Compton, Stanford Dingley, Brimpton, Yattendon, Brad-field, Bucklebury, Streatley, Alder-maston, Sonning, Bray, Wraysbury (8)	Lam-bourn, That-cham, Reading, Cookham Windsor	Reading, (Wickham) (9)		East Shefford, Aldworth, Southcote, Burgh-field, Earley

| | Found: | | | | | |
Ages (human):	Fields, farms (1):	Villages:	Towns:	Forts, castles (2):	Industry:	Other:
Roman	Lambourn, Kintbury, Box-ford, Hampstead Norreys, Hermitage, Aldermaston, Tidmarsh, Lower Basildon, Maidenhead, Cox Green	Wickham, Thatcham, Aldworth, Ufton Nervet, Reading, Finchampstead, Hurley, Knowl Hill	Silchester		Hamstead Marshall (6)	Newbury, Compton, Waltham St Lawrence (7)
Iron Age (3)	Thatcham, Reading, Arbor-field, Binfield, Maidenhead, Slough	(Speen) (5)	(Sil-chester) (5)	Padworth (4) — Membury, Coombe, Boxford, Hampstead Norreys, Chieveley, Cold Ash, Hermitage, Bracknell, Cox Green, Taplow	Thatcham, Arborfield (3)	

APPENDIX THREE: Archæological sites and exhibits

Ages (human):	Found:				
	Fields, farms (1):	Villages:	Towns:	Forts, castles (2):	Industry:	Other:
NOTES:					

(1) Initially, 'enclosed' areas of various kinds. Roman sites are all 'villas'.

(2) 'Hillforts' included, although most are now believed not to have had a warlike function.

(3) Two iron-working sites found near Thatcham (*see Chapter 8*), varying from 2,500 to 3,000 years BP. NB Caesar's Camp hillfort near Bracknell probably protected iron deposits. Arborfield may have continued to operate under the Romans.

(4) Pre-Roman fortifications near Silchester: Catuvellaunian site of Calleva?

(5) Some late Iron Age towns and villages can be inferred from Roman reports, but evidence of them has not been found.

(6) Pottery kilns.

(7) Although the general line followed by Roman roads is often known, only one Roman milestone has been found (at Finchampstead) and routes are generally inferred from small stretches that have been found. The sites listed here are cemeteries (Newbury) and temples (Lowbury Hill, near Compton and Weycock Hill, near Waltham St Lawrence).

(8) Several villages are inferred from evidence of a Saxon church.

(9) The church may have been fortified; it may also have carried a beacon.

(10) Potteries and a brickworks (Slough).

(11) Reading Abbey, the Bishop of Salisbury's Palace at Sonning. A large number of churches and monastic establishments of different kinds were founded in the twelfth and thirteenth centuries CE.

Appendix Four

Directions to sites mentioned in this book

MUCH USEFUL INFORMATION relating to many of these sites is available on the Berkshire Geoconservation website, https://berksgeoconservation.org.uk, accessed 3 May 2021. They are not always easy to find…

Site:	Chapter:	Directions:	Notes:
Berkshire syncline, southern rim	Cover	Going east on the A4, layby just past petrol station after Woolhampton	Footpath up hill, from opposite corner of petrol station
Dry Sandford nature reserve	2	A34 to Abingdon; A415 westwards; north (signposted Shippon, Cothill, Frilford Heath); east on Black Horse Lane; after passing through Cothill,look for a sign and small car park on your right	Two old stone pits, many minor workings, outstanding fen
Bungum Lane, Inkpen	3	A4 to just east of Hungerford; south through Inkpen towards Ham and Shalbourne; after church look for second bridleway on the left	Narrow road; parking for at most one small car; or see Inkpen walk *in Chapter 8*

Site:	Chapter:	Directions:	Notes:
Cookham Dean chalk pit	3	North along A404 from M4 junction; south at roundabout, along A308; from Pinkneys Green, follow signposts to Winterhill; after King's Coppice farm look for parking (or follow Cookham Dean walk *in Chapter 8*)	You may have to park in the village and walk back (take a map); the site is a little way from the back of the farm buildings up a footpath by the National Trust sign
Lynch Wood winterbourne	3	B4000 to Lambourn; Big Lane; Lynch Lane (park where you can without blocking residents); wood is in front of you	Only one real path in; springs are 50 to 100 metres from where path enters wood
Owl Pit (chalk pit)	3, 5	North out of Stanford Dingley; east along Back Lane, past Rushall Farm; north on to Scratchface Lane; look for the pit and parking for two cars on your right	
Pincent's Kiln SSSI	4	Following the A4 into Reading from M4, Junction 12 take the first ('superstore') exit and follow Pincent's Lane past IKEA to Pincent's Kiln Industrial Park on your right; the SSSI is next to Specialised Paintwork	It may be best to park at the multistorey by IKEA and walk up; there is a little on-street parking a long way up Pincent's Lane

Site:	Chapter:	Directions:	Notes:
Chapel Farm (sarsens)	4	North out of Newbury along B4494; east at crossroads to Peasemore and Beedon; look for the farm on your right; probably room for two cars without blocking farm access	In the farm-yard, look for sign then follow bridle-way for 150 metres or so
The Coombes	4	West out of Wokingham along the B3030; south on to Bearwood Road, to Barkham; west into Coombes Lane (park where you can without blocking residents)	Look for finger-post on the left: circular walk and many good paths
The Devil's Highway	4	A329(M) to Bracknell; at roundabout, south along A3095; at roundabout, south-west along B3348	No places to stop, and only parking well short of Devil's Highway, but footpaths from parking cut across; outcrop is just before Highway enters underpass below A3095
Lough Down (Goring Gap)	5	North-east along B4009; as you enter Streatley, look for small parking place on left	Limited parking, no alter-natives; time your visit with this in mind
Quarry Wood (Thames terraces)	5	North along A404 from M4; at roundabout, south along A308; from Pinkneys Green, follow signposts to Winter-hill; at Bisham Wood look for parking	Several paths lead towards front of down; you will know the viewpoint when you reach it

Site:	Chapter:	Directions:	Notes:
Winter Hill (Thames terraces)	5	As for Quarry Wood; at Bisham Wood (no signpost), turn right and look for signpost on left; road is very narrow	Some parking at viewpoint; best visited in winter (trees obstruct view at other times)
Shurlock Row (iron pan)	6	South from Maidenhead along A330; west on B3018, follow signposts for Shurlock Row; continue through village (across junction at green) and look for second footpath on left (Wick's Lane)	A little parking at end of Wick's Lane (park considerately); follow lane southwards; a few pieces of iron pan visible in path and on verge, once past final farm
Hogmoor Field (periglacial landforms)	8	North along A340 from A4; after crossing M4, look for small, discreet turning on right; see Sulham walk *in Chapter 8*	Moor Copse reserve car park is small; may be busy at weekends
Bucklebury Ford	Cover	West from Reading along A4; follow signposts for Bucklebury (three right turns and over a crossroad); in village park at recreation ground	Walk back to church; take footpath through churchyard and paddock beyond; follow road over bridge and right at junction; in ¼ mile, turn right on to bridleway

Other sites, for which I have not included photographs, are listed below:

Site:	Directions:	Notes:
Berkshire syncline, north-western rim	Informal car parks and pull-in spots on both sides of B4494, near junction with Ridgeway path	
Lambourn Seven Barrows	North-west along B4000 from Newbury; in Lambourn, north on to B4001; at fork take left (Wantage Lane); right on to track; park through gate to your left	For track, watch out for a small sign at a Y-junction
Radley Bottom (dry valley)	North out of Hungerford along A338; east at second crossroads (The Tally Ho), towards North Denford and Avington	Places to stop (but not park), and some footpaths; this road better for driving or cycling than for walking
Winterbourne Chalk Pit SSSI	North along B4494 from Newbury; just before M4, turn south-west to Winterbourne; take first right and first right after that; follow bridleway past St James-the-Less church, and park at farm (without blocking gates or tracks)	On land owned by Lower Farm; ask permission and directions
Gough's Lane Newt Reserve	From A322, follow A3095 north through Bracknell; once it becomes Warfield Road, turn west on to Holly Spring Lane and almost immediately north on to Gough's Lane; after Enborne Gardens, park and look for sign on left	Lovely, small nature reserve at which Bagshot sand, and (a little) London clay can be seen

Site:	Directions:	Notes:
Hurley swallow hole	North along A404 from M4; at roundabout, south-west to Burchetts Green; on leaving village, first left (Honey Lane) and look for parking by footpath on left; take footpath uphill; turn right immediately after tumble-down fence; path crosses road at Ladyeplace Cottages; swallow hole is after third kissing gate	Swallow hole, at junction of Lambeth Group and chalk, where stream flows into ground; parking for two small cars only (and very little in Burchetts Green)
Cocksherd Wood	North along A308 from M4; follow signs for A4 eastwards (Bridge Road); north on to Huntercombe Lane and north-east on to Priory Road, which becomes Lower Britwell Road; look for Dove House Crescent on right; park at far end and look for sign near its junction with Farnham Lane	Lovely, small wood at which Lambeth Group clay and sand can be seen, Lynch Hill gravel and several periglacial landforms; and in April, bluebells
Windsor	Parking in Windsor is tricky; it may be best to go by train (to Windsor and Eton Riverside)	Only fleeting views of pericline can be seen from Home Park, and then in winter (because of extensive tree planting)

Glossary

age   **Epochs** are divided into ages, some of which are divided into sub-ages; *see Appendix 2*

aquifer   A body of rock, **sand** or gravel through which large amounts of water move; it may be capable of storing water

archæology   Human (and proto-human) activity in the recent and distant past can be studied through what humans (and proto-humans) left behind them

asthenosphere
               The hotter, more ductile zone of the mantle, below the **lithosphere**

bedrock   Layers that are deep and/or old enough to have lithified (turned partly or wholly into stone); a convenient, but imprecise name

boulder   **Clast** above 256mm in diameter

clast   Fragments of rock ranging from **boulders** to **silt grains** in size; may be angular (sometimes used as shorthand for showing one or more broken face) or rounded (e.g. by transport in water); a convenient, but imprecise name

clay   **Grain** less than 0.002mm in diameter (NB chemists say 0.001mm, soil scientists say 0.0039mm)

cobble   **Clast** between 64 and 256mm in diameter

conservative plate boundary
               Where one plate slides past another

constructive plate boundary
               Where two plates move apart and **magma** is drawn up into the gap, creating new surface

destructive plate boundary
Where one plate is **subducted** beneath another and recycled

eon
The (estimated) 4,500 million years of Earth's history is divided into three Precambrian eons and the current, Phanerozoic, eon (last 544 million years); Phanerozoic comes from two Greek words meaning 'visible life' – *see Appendix 2*

epoch
Periods are divided into epochs – *see Appendix 2*

era
The Phanerozoic **eon** is divided into three eras: the Palæozoic (ancient life) from 544 million years ago, the Mesozoic (middle life) from 245 million years ago and the Cenozoic (recent life), the last 65 million years – *see Appendix 2*

fault
A place where the rock has broken and one or both sides of the break have moved; *see* **normal fault, reverse fault** and **transcurrent fault**

formation
Formations are divided into **members** and may be collected into **groups**

graben
Parallel splits, between which an area of rock sinks; like a wedge falling when its two neighbours move apart; *see* **horst**

grain
Individual particles of **sand, silt** and **clay** tend to be called grains rather than **clasts**

group
A category of rocks and other layers clearly different from those above and below; may contain several **formations**

horst
Parallel splits, between which an area of rock rises; like a wedge being pushed up when its two neighbours move together; *see* **graben**

inlier
An area of rock surrounded by much younger beds; *see* **outlier**

K–Pg boundary
: Boundary between the Cretaceous and Palæogene **periods**; often marked by a thin layer of dark clay containing iridium; a mass-extinction event

lithosphere
: A convenient way of describing the crust and the upper 100km or so of the mantle, which in many ways act together

lithostratigraphy
: Drawing or describing (–graphy) layers (–strat(a)i–) of rock (litho–); distinguishing and identifying the successive layers of rock, **sand**, **clay** and soil in an area, which may be small or large

loess
: Drifts of fine-grained material built up by winds in cold, dry periods of or after an Ice Age

magma
: Molten igneous rock, while it is still in the ground; after it has been erupted it is known as lava

marl
: A fine sediment, typically laid down in deep water; may be made up largely of microfossils; may appear in layers between **clays**, **silts**, **sands**, etc.

massif
: A very large block, usually composed of different, harder rock than its surroundings

member
: A **formation** may be divided into members: rocks and other layers distinct from other members in the formation

normal fault
: Where rock has broken and one side of the break has fallen; *see* **reverse fault** and **transcurrent fault**

orogeny
: Mountain ranges created when continents collide

outcrop
: Rock visible at the surface

outlier
: An area of rock surrounded by much older beds; *see* **inlier**

palæomagnetism
> When rocks are formed they record the polarity of the world at that time (i.e. direction of the North and South magnetic poles); since both poles move (indeed, North and South polarity have occasionally switched) a rock's palæomagnetism can tell us roughly where or when it formed

pebble
> **Clast** between 2mm and 64mm in diameter

pericline
> A concentric fold; where convex (as at Windsor) they typically have an older core surrounded with later layers

periglacial
> Strictly, an area next to a glacier; more usually, an environment characterised by long periods of freezing (even permafrost) followed by long periods of thaw

period
> **Eras** are divided into periods – *see Appendix 2*

reverse fault
> Where rock has broken and one side of the break has risen; *see* **normal fault** and **transcurrent fault**

sand
> **Grain** between 0.62 and 2mm in diameter

sill
> Where rock has split and **magma** has filled the gap; originally flat or slightly inclined (though later ground movements may tilt sills upwards)

silt
> **Grain** between 0.002 and 0.62mm in diameter

subduction
> Where gravity or convection drags plates towards each other, the lighter passes over the heavier, which is subducted back into the mantle

superficial deposits
> Usually, soil or (comparatively) recent deposits that have not lithified (turned to stone): in Berkshire, these can include **periglacial** deposits, peat, **silt**, **clay**, **sands** and extensive gravel beds, both along

rivers and on ridge-tops

syncline   A concave fold, typically having an older rim and filled with later layers

tectonics   From the Greek word *tekton*, this means 'building' or 'structure'; plate tectonics is the theory that describes how the movement of geological plates explains the structure of the Earth

transcurrent fault
              'Transcurrent', or 'strike-slip', or 'transform' (US terminology) describes parallel movement in opposite directions; *see* **normal fault** and **reverse fault**

unconformity Where layers are present in neighbouring areas but either were never laid down in Berkshire, or have been eroded away

References

General reference

Berkshire Geoconservation (2019), https://berksgeoconservation.org.uk, accessed 10 June 2019

Grotzinger, John P. and Thomas H. Jordan (2014), *Understanding Earth*, seventh edition (New York: W.H. Freeman/Macmillan Education)

Park, Graham (2012), *Introducing Tectonics, Rock Structures and Mountain Belts* (Edinburgh: Dunedin Academic Press)

Rothery, David A. (2017), *Geology: A complete introduction*, revised edition (London: John Murray Learning/Hodder & Stoughton)

More specialised

Aldiss, D.T. (2012), 'The stratigraphical framework for the Palæogene successions of the London Basin, UK', British Geological Survey Open Report OR/12/004 (Keyworth, Notts: British Geological Survey)

Berkshire Geoconservation Group (2019), leaflets and factsheets available online at https://berksgeoconservation.org.uk/reports.php, specifically:
Dunlop, Lesley (ed.) (2019), 'Building materials of Berkshire'
Dunlop, Lesley (ed.) (2009), 'Gravels of Berkshire: origin, history, industry & recreation'
and accompanying fact sheets: 'Gravels of Berkshire: West Berkshire, Reading, Wokingham, Bracknell Forest, Windsor and Maidenhead, Slough'

Berkshire Record Office (2020), 'Understanding enclosure: the distribution of enclosure in Berkshire', available online at www.berkshireenclosure.org.uk/background_temporal.asp, accessed 7 March 2020

Bridgland, D.R. and P.L. Gibbard (1997), 'Quaternary river diversions in the London Basin and the eastern English Channel', *Géographie physique et Quaternaire* **51**(3), 337–46

British Geological Survey, 1:50,000 scale geological maps, sheets 255, 267, 268, 269, 283 and 284; 'Berkshire mineral resources', available at www.bgs.ac.uk/downloads/start.cfm?id=2590, accessed 14 February 2020

British Geological Survey, BGS Lexicon of Named Rock Units, available at https://webapps.bgs.ac.uk/lexicon/home.cfm, accessed 26 October 2020

Brown, Ian (2009), *Beacons in the Landscape: The Hillforts of England and Wales* (Oxford: Windgather Press)

Burt, Stephen (2010), 'Berkshire's extreme weather over the decades', available at http://news.bbc.co.uk/local/berkshire/hi/people_and_places/nature/newsid_8983000/8983809.stm#:~:text=Berkshire%20is%20wetter%20in%20the,county%20averages%20less%20than%20600mm., accessed 14 November 2020

Carlile, Michael (2005), 'The red streams of East Berkshire' in Michael J. Crawley (ed.), *The Flora of Berkshire* (Harpenden: Brambleby Books)

Chartres, C.J. (1981), 'The mineralogy of Quaternary deposits in the Kennet valley, Berkshire', *Proceedings of the Geologists Association* **92**(2), 93–103

Clarke, M.R. and A.J. Dixon (1981), 'The Pleistocene braided river deposits in the Blackwater valley area of Berkshire and Hampshire, England', *Proceedings of the Geologists Association* **92**(2), 139–57

Dinnis, Rob and Chris Stringer (2015), *Britain: One Million Years of the Human Story*, revised edn (London: Natural History Museum)

English Heritage (1991), *Exploring our Past: Strategies for the Archaeology of England* (London: Her Majesty's Stationery Office)

Entwisle, D.C., P.R.N. Hobbs, K.J. Northmore, J. Skipper, M.R. Raines, S.J. Self, R.A. Ellison and L.D. Jones (2013), *Engineering Geology of British Rocks and Soils – Lambeth Group* (Keyworth, Notts: British Geological Survey)

Foster, D., D.W. Holliday, C.M. Jones, B. Owens and A. Welsh (1989), 'The concealed Upper Palæozoic rocks of Berkshire and south Oxfordshire', *Proceedings of the Geologists' Association* **100**(3), 395–407

Fulford, Michael (2017), 'Silchester Roman Town', Guidebook (London: English Heritage)

Gale, A.S., P.A. Jeffrey, J.M. Huggett and P. Connolly (1999), 'Eocene inversion history of the Sandown Pericline, Isle of Wight, Southern England', *Journal of the Geological Society* 156, 327–39

Gibbard, Philip and John Lewin (2003), 'History of the major rivers of southern Britain during the Tertiary', *Journal of the Geological Society* 160, 829–45

Greene, Kevin and Tom Moore (2010), *Archæology: An Introduction*, 5th edn (Abingdon: Routledge)

Greenhalgh, Tate and Lisa Hendry (2017), 'Human evolution – the making of an island', Natural History Museum, available online at www.nhm.ac.uk/discover/the-making-of-an-island.html, accessed 27 August 2019

Hansen, David L., Derek J. Blundell and Søren B. Nielsen (2002), 'A model for the evolution of the Weald Basin', *Bulletin of the Geological Society of Denmark* 49, 109–18

Healy, F., M. Heaton, S.J. Lobb, M.J. Allen, I.M. Fenwick, R. Grace and R.G. Scaife (1992), 'Excavations of a Mesolithic site at Thatcham, Berkshire', *Proceedings of the Prehistoric Society* **58**(1), 41

Historic England (nd), 'Heritage Gateway', available online at www.heritagegateway.org.uk/gateway/, accessed 28 April 2021

Kemp, S.J. and D. Wagner (2006), 'The mineralogy, geochemistry and surface area of mudrocks from the London Clay Formation of southern England', British Geological Survey Physical Hazards Programme Internal Report IR/06/060 (Keyworth, Notts: British Geological Survey)

Lambrick, Gabriella (1969), 'Some old roads of north Berkshire', *Oxoniensia* XXXIV, 78–93

Lewin, J. and P.L. Gibbard (2010), 'Quaternary river terraces in England: forms, sediments and processes', *Geomorphology* **120**(3–4), 293–311

Lock, G. and I. Ralston (2017), 'Atlas of hillforts of Britain and Ireland', available online at https://hillforts.arch.ox.ac.uk/, accessed 23 February 2021

Mainstone, C.P. (ed.) (1999), 'Chalk rivers: nature conservation and management', for English Nature and The Environment Agency (Medmenham: Water Research Centre)

McMillan, Andrew and Jonathan Merritt (2012), 'A new Quaternary and Neogene lithostratigraphical framework for Great Britain and the Isle of Man', *Proceedings of the Geologists' Association* **123**(4), 679–91

McMillan, A.A., R.J.O. Hamblin and J.W. Merritt (2011), *A Lithostratigraphical Framework for onshore Quaternary and Neogene (Tertiary) Superficial Deposits of Great Britain and the Isle of Man*, British Geological Survey Research Report RR/10/03 (Keyworth, Notts: British Geological Survey)

Nash Ford, David (nd), Royal Berkshire History, available at www.berkshirehistory.com, accessed 7 March 2020

Newell, Andrew, James Sorensen, Jonathan Chambers, Paul Wilkinson, Sebastian Uhlemann, Colin Roberts, Darren Gooddy, Christopher Vane and Andrew Binley (2015), 'Fluvial response to late Pleistocene and Holocene environmental change in a Thames chalkland headwater: the Lambourn of southern England', *Proceedings of the Geologists' Association* **126**(5), 683–97

Oxford Archæology (2007), 'Solent Thames Research Framework', available online at https://oxfordarchaeology.com/research-publication/solent-thames-research-framework/county-assessments, accessed 22 February 2020: specifically,

Hosfield, Robert (2007), 'Lower/Middle Palæolithic, Berkshire'

Chisham, Catherine (2006), 'The Upper Palæolithic and Mesolithic of Berkshire'

Ford, Steve (2007a), 'Neolithic and early Bronze Age Berkshire'

Ford, Steve (2007b), 'Later Bronze Age and Iron Age Berkshire'

Greenaway, Jill (2006), 'Roman Berkshire'

Clark, Steve (2007), 'Early Medieval Berkshire (AD410–1066)'

Astill, Grenville (2006), 'Medieval Berkshire, c. 1000–1600'

Hopkins, David (2006), 'Post Medieval and Modern (Industrial, Military, Institutions and Designed Landscapes) Hampshire and Berkshire'

Oxfordshire Geology Trust (nd), 'Fact sheet: chalk and groundwater'

Rawson, P.F., P.M. Allen and A.S. Gale (2001), 'The Chalk Group – a revised lithostratigraphy', *Geoscientist* **11**, 21

Sharples, Niall (2006), 'Building communities and creating identities in the first millennium BC' in Colin Haselgrove and Rachel Pope (eds), *The Earlier Iron Age in Britain and the Near Continent* (Oxford: Oxbow)

Shindler, Karolyn (2014), 'Colonising Britain – one million years of our human story', *Current Archaeology* **288**, available online at www.archaeology.co.uk/articles/features/colonising-britain-one-million-years-of-our-human-story.htm, accessed 27 August 2019

Sumbler, M.G. (ed.) (1996), *British Regional Geology: London and the Thames Valley*, 4th edn (London: Her Majesty's Stationery Office)

Swan, Vivien (nd), 'The pottery kilns of Roman Britain', available online at https://romankilns.net/, accessed 7 March 2020

Thatcham: www.thatchamtowncouncil.gov.uk/thatcham/history-of-the-town/

Toghill, Peter (2000), *The Geology of Britain: An Introduction* (my copy: Marlborough: Crowood Press, 2012)

Ullyott, J. Stewart, David J. Nash, Colin A. Whiteman and Rory N. Mortimore (2004), 'Distribution, petrology and mode of development of silcretes (sarsens and puddingstones) on the eastern South Downs, UK', *Earth Surfaces, Processes and Landforms* **29**(12), 1509–39

Weber, Karrie A., Laurie A. Achenbach and John D. Coates (2006), 'Microorganisms pumping iron: anaerobic microbial iron oxidation and reduction', *Nature Reviews Microbiology* 4, 752–64

White, Mark, Beccy Scott and Nick Ashton (2006), 'The early middle Palæolithic in Britain: archæology, settlement history and human behaviour', *Journal of Quaternary Science* 21, 525

Wymer, John (1999), *The Lower Palæolithic Occupation of Britain*, vol. 2 *The Distribution Maps and Gazetteer of Sites* (Salisbury: Trust for Wessex Archæology)